# From the Peaceable

This book applies Thorstein Veblen's cultural theory to a qualitative study of the *charro* cowboy culture and community in Mexico. Drawing on Veblen's arguments regarding cultural lag, the peaceable and the barbaric, predatory culture, vested interest, and pecuniary interest, it examines the comportment, clothing, mannerisms, and adherence to the norms that are unique to this subculture, while considering the cultural changes within race, class, and gender dynamics of this community in relation to mainstream Mexico. With close attention to the impact of business principles and standardization on the *charro*, leading to changes in practices and social interactions, the author considers generational differences and the tensions that exist between newer and older *charros* as a result of the developing emphasis on business. A close study of the nature of cultural adaptability and the persistence of inequality regardless of mainstream illusions of equality, this volume sheds new light on our understanding of what culture *is* rather than what culture *does*, while reintroducing the neglected ethnographic streak in Veblen's work as an important methodological and theoretical tool in the interpretation of culture.

**Beatriz Aldana Marquez** is Assistant Professor in the Department of Sociology at Texas State University.

# Classical and Contemporary Social Theory

Classical and Contemporary Social Theory publishes rigorous scholarly work that re-discovers the relevance of social theory for contemporary times, demonstrating the enduring importance of theory for modern social issues. The series covers social theory in a broad sense, inviting contributions on both 'classical' and modern theory, thus encompassing sociology, without being confined to a single discipline. As such, work from across the social sciences is welcome, provided that volumes address the social context of particular issues, subjects, or figures and offer new understandings of social reality and the contribution of a theorist or school to our understanding of it.

The series considers significant new appraisals of established thinkers or schools, comparative works or contributions that discuss a particular social issue or phenomenon in relation to the work of specific theorists or theoretical approaches. Contributions are welcome that assess broad strands of thought within certain schools or across the work of a number of thinkers, but always with an eye toward contributing to contemporary understandings of social issues and contexts.

**Series Editor**
Stjepan G. Mestrovic, Texas A&M University, USA

**Freud as a Social and Cultural Theorist**
On Human Nature and the Civilizing Process
*Howard L. Kaye*

**From the Peaceable to the Barbaric**
Thorstein Veblen and the Charro Cowboy
*Beatriz Aldana Marquez*

**Morality Made Visible**
Edward Westermarck's Moral and Social Theory
*Otto Pipatti*

**Critical and Cultural Interactionism**
Insights from Sociology and Criminology
*Edited by Michael Hviid Jacobsen*

For more information about this series, please visit: https://www.routledge.com/sociology/series/ASHSER1383

# From the Peaceable to the Barbaric

## Thorstein Veblen and the Charro Cowboy

**Beatriz Aldana Marquez**

Routledge
Taylor & Francis Group

LONDON AND NEW YORK

First published 2019
by Routledge
2 Park Square, Milton Park, Abingdon, Oxon OX14 4RN

and by Routledge
52 Vanderbilt Avenue, New York, NY 10017

First issued in paperback 2020

*Routledge is an imprint of the Taylor & Francis Group, an informa business*

*British Library Cataloguing in Publication Data*
A catalogue record for this book is available from the British Library

*Library of Congress Cataloging-in-Publication Data*
Names: Aldana Marquez, Beatriz, author.
Title: From the peaceable to the barbaric : Thorstein Veblen and the charro
cowboy / Beatriz Aldana Marquez.
Description: Abingdon, Oxon ; New York, NY : Routledge, 2019. |
Series: Classical and contemporary social theory series |
Includes bibliographical references and index.
Identifiers: LCCN 2018049512|
ISBN 9781138498273 (hbk : alk. paper) | ISBN 9781351016599 (ebk)
Subjects: LCSH: Charros--Mexico. | Social classes--Mexico. |
Group identity--Mexico. | Veblen, Thorstein, 1857-1929.
Classification: LCC SF284.42.M6 A43 2019 | DDC 636.2--dc23
LC record available at https://lccn.loc.gov/2018049512

ISBN 13: 978-0-367-66118-2 (pbk)
ISBN 13: 978-1-138-49827-3 (hbk)

Typeset in Times New Roman
by Taylor & Francis Books

# Contents

# 1 Introduction

Thorstein Veblen's cultural analysis has been used in the areas of culture and economics to explain differences in consumption based on social class. While Veblen's most recognized theory, conspicuous consumption, is widely used in sociology, Veblen's other vast contributions remain predominantly unknown and unused by cultural theorists in sociology. The aim of this book is to connect Veblen's contributions using the case study of the charro (Mexican cowboy, which I will refer to as the charro cowboy) community. This community can be defined as a specific type of Mexican rural culture originating from the colonial period that later formed into a rodeo type of culture. While this work extends beyond the Untied States, it validates Veblen's theory as transcending beyond American borders and can be useful to explore and investigate changing social cultural phenomena. The charro cowboy tradition, the national sport of Mexico, serves as the personification of centuries of culture and tradition as it is displayed through comportment and clothing, as well as the behavior, mannerisms, and adherence to the norms that are unique to this subculture. The charro cowboy community serves as an ideal case study of Veblen's conception of the peaceable to the barbaric due to the growing influence of business principles. Although the charro cowboy tradition has changed throughout the years, Veblen's theories can help document the cultural changes within race, class, and gender of this community in relation to mainstream Mexico, making his theories relevant to current ethnographic analyses.

Thorstein Veblen (1857–1929) was a Norwegian-American social theorist who is simultaneously praised as America's greatest social critic and largely forgotten in the social sciences. He has been labeled variously as an economist, sociologist, and social critic. But according to his biographer, Joseph Dorfman, he devoted most of his time at the University of Chicago to studies of ethnographies and anthropology. But he is not cited by contemporary anthropologists or ethnographers. I propose to develop and apply this neglected ethnographic part of Veblen's social theory, with regard to both theory and methodology. Like his contemporaries, Durkheim and Westermarck, Veblen developed an evolutionary theory of culture based upon extensive ethnographic research. The key points of his theory are that ancient barbaric traits are carried over into modern traits of conspicuous consumption, waste, and leisure; that the barbaric status of women as trophies is transformed but not eliminated in modern cultures; and that the "dolicho-blond" (white) cultural group carries predatory habits from the past into the present and future. I will illustrate these points, among others, in my ethnography of the charro cowboy community in contemporary Mexico.

## Plan of the book

In Chapter 1, I provide a brief historical overview of Thorstein Veblen's theoretical framework beyond his theory of conspicuous consumption. Additionally, I will offer a brief biographical sketch of his life and times based primarily upon Joseph Dorfman's book, *Thorstein Veblen and His America* (1934), as well as David Riesman's (1953) intellectual biography of Veblen. Veblen's cultural understanding, ultimately forgotten by cultural sociologists, can be understood in terms of contamination of the original intentions of a particular culture and demonstrate their utility throughout the remainder of this book. I merge the contributions of his various works to explain why his reasoning presents the best explanation in the examination of changes in rural cultures, as in the charro cowboy tradition, exposed to features of the capitalistic spirit, rapid urbanization, and the pressure to use modern technology. Culture in this book will not be examined by differences in stages, such as developmental, but rather differences in kind. In this chapter, I also briefly delineate the complex history of the Mexican charro cowboy to familiarize the reader with its cultural significance and highlight the limitations of previous qualitative work on the charro cowboy community. Cultural shifts in the charro cowboy community are not uniform and emerge through careful examination that can only be clearly viewed through Veblen's paradigm. Social structures within the bounds of the charro cowboy tradition designating gender relations, class dynamics, and distinctions regarding skin color resonate with Veblen's arguments regarding cultural lag, the peaceable and the barbaric, predatory culture, vested interest, and pecuniary interests. To conclude I explain the significance of my ethnographic methodological approach and my connection to the charro cowboy community.

Chapter 2 examines Veblen's theory of business principles as it relates to the growing capitalistic spirit of the charro cowboy community. This chapter introduces the concept of the charro cowboy *jefe* or the charro cowboy boss, operating like a bank, holding executive power over charro teams. The charro cowboy *jefe* is the owner of a charro cowboy team, solely responsible for winning competition titles, prizes, and recognition. Due to the growing pressure to win competitions, charro competitions have become more standardized than ever before and the safety of both animals and competitors has been compromised. I argue that the changing nature of the charro cowboy community, primarily the growing emphasis on business principles, has resulted in a growing rift between the new generation and older generations of charro men.

Chapter 3 analyses the socialization process of the charro cowboy with generational ties and their charro rookie counterparts using Veblen's *Theory of the Leisure Class* (1899) to address class and racial differences. Generational ties become a symbolic mechanism of distinction between authentic connections to the charro cowboy tradition. I highlight the subtle way in which lower class charros use these generational ties to negotiate their legitimacy against wealthier members. The emphasis on "bloodline" as the only true component in "belonging" to the charro cowboy tradition will be the most used mechanism of defense among the younger and older generations of charro cowboys. While the older generation of charro cowboys are more likely to express that authenticity is dependent upon generational ties, the younger generation of charro cowboys with generational ties will make an effort to be more inclusive to outsiders or charro rookies. However, these expressions of inclusivity are dependent on the audience. Ultimately, I argue that charro rookies with indigenous ties experience higher incidents of marginalization and acts of exclusion from generational charro cowboys, regardless of age, further displaying the contradictions of the original intentions of charro cowboy brotherhood.

In the following two chapters I focus my attention on the role of women in the charro cowboy community. In Chapter 4, Veblen's *The Barbarian Status of Women* (1899) is used to demonstrate how women in the charro cowboy community are continuously marginalized. The role of women in the cowboy community is reinforced and reproduced throughout generations of both men and women. Women in the charro cowboy community can be separated into different categories: 1) charro cowboy female family members; 2) charro cowboy love interests; and 3) female outsiders, *vendedoras*. I argue that this hierarchy of women in the charro cowboy community also plays a role in how women are "respected" and approached by charro cowboys. Further, the chapter explores the socialization of women in the charro cowboy community from generational ties compared to non-generational ties. The chapter also notes the important differences between these categories and illustrates how some women who resist charro cowboy culture are often and forcibly maneuvered back into submission.

Chapter 5 reflects upon the role of *escaramuzas* or charro cowboy women in competition. The main focus of this chapter is that *escaramuzas* tend to have a high income, generational ties, and are seen as respectable members of the charro cowboy community in comparison to other women in the charro cowboy community. Using both *The Barbarian Status of Women* (1899) and *The Theory of Leisure Class* (1899), *escaramuzas* can be classified as the ultimate form of symbolic conspicuous waste due to the vast economic investment that is needed to participate and organize competitions. Their contemporary competitions lack the same historical ties to equestrian skill of charro cowboy competitions. *Escaramuzas* are examined as a separate component in charro cowboy competitions and I document how these women view themselves in comparison to their charro cowboy male counterparts. Further, the chapter demonstrates how the Mexican Federation of Charros view *escaramuzas* as a way of making additional money, revealing their true vested interest in maintaining its tradition, even though *escaramuzas* hold no representative power in the Federation. Lastly, the chapter argues that charro cowboy women, even the most prestigious, are marginalized despite their fundamental role in charro cowboy history.

Chapter 6 returns to the larger societal context of Veblen's theoretical contributions in cultural sociology. The logic of the charro cowboy tradition might seem irrational to outsiders, however, with careful consideration and appropriate cultural and theoretical framework, these irrationalities become much clearer. I argue that the charro cowboy tradition, analysed through the understanding of Veblen's cultural logic, will continue to undergo change as long as Mexican society grows as a nation. The existing gatekeepers of the charro cowboy tradition will ultimately work hard to maintain components of the tradition as long as people remain active participants. In this concluding chapter, I address the implications of this book to scholars of Veblen's work and encourage current and future ethnographers to incorporate his work in their assessments of culture.

Thorstein Veblen, often characterized as a quick-witted critic of capitalism, is recognized for his contribution to economic theory and sociological thought. Although a controversial figure, his most popular work, *The Theory of the Leisure Class*, demonstrates the changes in society that manifest social goods as evidence of wealth, power, and status. Nevertheless, this popular piece of work is not his only worthwhile contribution. Veblen remains popular with his followers, against his own wishes. In his critical biography of Veblen, David Riesman (1953, pp. 2–3) stated, "Veblen left strict instructions in his will that no biography or other memorial of him be prepared—but fortunately these instructions were disregarded by his admirers." Although Veblen was highly respected by his admirers, his contributions often remain marginal to cultural sociologists. Veblen's controversial personal history and social theories may have derailed his career, nevertheless, the value of Veblen's work is timeless and essential to the analysis of cultural settings. A son of a Norwegian farming family, Veblen's immigrant and rural background provided the necessary basis for his understanding of social theories such as innovation and parental bent, which refers to the genuine instinct to nurture and care for society (Riesman 1953). This chapter aims to review Veblen's importance to the scholarship of economics, sociology, and most importantly cultural examination. Further, I will argue for the use of Veblen's scholarship in the analysis of Mexico's oldest equestrian tradition, the charro cowboy tradition, highlighting Veblen's own use of qualitative observations to support his theoretical assertions.

Joseph's Dorfman's *Thorstein Veblen and his America*, a detailed and the most comprehensive biography of Veblen's life, clearly highlights the influences in the development of Veblen's scholarship. This is evident throughout explanations of his transition from his humble Norwegian background to his educational experiences. Veblen left his family farm and was separated from his cultural frame of reference. This is often the case for individuals that experience cultural shock when attending an institution of higher learning. When describing Veblen's earlier experiences in Baltimore, Dorfman (1934) wrote:

At Baltimore Veblen found himself in the culture of the South, with its highly developed leisure class. For a while he was a boarder in a family which still clung to its aristocratic traditions. The raw youth was much amused by the family's maintenance of the grand old pre-war style, with servants and meals which cost far more than was received from boarders.

(p. 38)

Examples, like the one above, demonstrate how Veblen's academic journey from farmland to ivy league campus played a major role in how Veblen was able to develop and form his theories and interpretation of American life, especially in his observation of the wealthy and highly educated classes. While Veblen did not deliberately use examples from his personal biography in his work, Dorfman's outline of Veblen's life provides the clear connection.

Another example can be observed in Veblen's response to Mile Levasseur, a follower of the classical school of economics. In his book on American agriculture, Levasseur argued that American farmers' complaints were, "not altogether well grounded". Levasseur originally argued, along with others, that the disadvantages of the American farmer could be solved by lowering rent to reflect the true value of the land. Veblen responded, with true Veblenian wit, by stating that Levasseur's opinion of the future of American agriculture is "hopeful without being enthusiastic" and pointing out the flaws of Levasseur's logic utilizing his agricultural experience and his own development of a "workable socialistic economics" that accounted for changes in economic phenomena. His critiques, while off-putting for individuals unfamiliar with Veblen's eccentric personality, were valid points because he disavowed economic theories that remained constant despite their inability to speak to changes in society.

Dorfman described Veblen's early career as presenting some difficulties, however, the most significant point that gives substance to the idea of Veblen as a qualitative observer is evident in his commentary after Veblen's appointment renewal at the University of Chicago. He provides accounts that show that Veblen himself admitted to being influenced by his experiences and observations. Dorfman stated:

In 1899, a month after the appearance of "The Barbarian Status of Women," the last of his *Journal* article, Veblen published his first book, *The Theory of the Leisure Class: An Economic Study in the Evolution of Institutions.* He told Stuart that the general ideas of the book had been formed in his boyhood, in large part by his father's remarks, and "Some Neglected Points in the Theory of Socialism" bears testimony that the book had been brewing in his mind before he came to Chicago.

(p.174)

Veblen's notions such as conspicuous consumption, conspicuous leisure, and pecuniary emulation were theorized by abstracting and carefully observing the occurrences of the society he lived in. As an outsider, to both his peers and ultimately his own family due his social mobility, Veblen had a talent for observing and making sense of social structures around him. Additionally, Dorfman wrote:

> The data, Veblen declared in the preface, "have been preference been drawn from everyday life, by direct observation or through common notoriety, rather than from more recondite sources as a farther remove." The introductory chapter presents the "theoretical premises" of the book. A more explicit statement of its theoretical position is made in the series of papers published in *The American Journal of Sociology*, "but the argument does not rest on these—in part novel—generalizations in such a way that it would altogether lose its possible value as a detail of economic theory in case these novel generalizations should, in the reader's apprehension, fall away through being insufficiently backed by author or data."
>
> (p. 175)

While Veblen's harsher critics protested against his use of observational data and terminology, his supporters were able to see beyond the embedded satire to the valuable cultural analysis. Qualitative work can bridge the gap between theory and application. Veblen was able to do both to provide explanations for cultural phenomena, especially in a context that his followers could understand.

Veblen's clear examples, pulled from observation, provided a straightforward depiction of a changing American society, but may have been too radical for classical economic scholars and early sociologists of culture. Veblen had an innovative approach to economics and sociological observations of culture that were underestimated by some of his colleagues and critics. While Veblen was fired in 1906 from the University of Chicago, prior to the emergence of the Chicago School during the 1920s, Veblen's assessment of culture held the same ethnographic spirit as his cultural sociology successors. Sidney Plotkin, a leading Veblen scholar, argued, "Veblen could not have been who he was without his remarkable, energizing encounter with the anthropology of his day. It is a good time for him to be returning the gift and for ethnographers to study actual the new deals of many capitalist places and times" (Plotkin 2017, 181). While anthropological ethnographic studies hold distinct academic schools of thought, the emergence of sociological ethnographies, as we know it, was still marginal. However, ethnography as a method was valuable to Veblen. Veblen was interested in economics, sociology, and philosophy, but it cannot be denied that Veblen was also interested in ethnographic approaches. Veblen's critical and qualitative dissection of the behavior of the upper class or the leisure class in an increasingly materialistic society singled out the realities of current values corrupted by financial motives.

C. Wright Mills argued that Thorstein Veblen was the foremost critic of America that America has ever produced. In the forward of Veblen's 1953 edition of *The Theory of the Leisure Class*, Mills stated, "We might learn from [Veblen] that the object of all social study is to understand the types of men and women that are selected and shaped by a given society—and to judge them by explicit standards." While Mills attributed Veblen's theory to an American economic context, Mestrovic (2003) interprets Veblen as a valid cultural theorist even if mainstream social and cultural theorists have ignored Veblen's contributions. Mestrovic (2003) states, "Rather than treat Veblen as he has been approached, as an economist, social critic, and problematic sociologist, I offer a new vision of him as a cultural theorist... [Veblen] concerned himself with topics that concern students of culture: fashion, leisure, work, education, the status of women, and other topics." While mainstream social and cultural theorists like Talcott Parsons, Jürgen Habermas, Anthony Giddens, Zygmunt Bauman, Robert Park, Everett Burgess, and George Ritzer marginalize Veblen's contributions, Riesman (1953) wrote an intellectual biography of Veblen in which he extends Veblen's significance as a cultural theorist beyond America and Veblen's milieu to international cultural settings. Riesman argues that Veblen's theory may be refracted in various historical and cultural contexts, including our own.

Veblen's *The Theory of the Leisure Class* (1899) may be his most famous and most cited scholarly work however it is not his only significant contribution. Veblen's *The Barbarian Status of Women* (1899), *The Vested Interest and the Common Man* (1920), *The Instinct of Workmanship and the State of the Industrial Arts (1914), The Theory of Business Enterprise* (1904), and *On the Nature and Uses of Sabotage* (1919) provide starting points to assessment of cultural phenomena. This collection of scholarship address issues such as gender inequality, class inequality, commodification, and the inconsistencies of Marxism. John Diggins, a distinguished professor of history, argued in his book, *Thorstein Veblen: Theorist of the Leisure Class* (1899), "Veblen deeply admired the 'boldness of conception' and 'great logical consistency' in Marx's writings. He therefore wanted first to defend Marx's writing. He therefore wanted first to defend Marx against his contemporary critics and then to show where the hidden flaw in Marxism actually lay" (Diggins 1999, 45). While Veblen accepted some aspects of Marxism, his theories provided a necessary cultural extension to the understanding of this economic theory.

Veblen's cultural theoretical framework is the most appropriate to document economic transitions of rural cultural institutions. The basic ingredient of Veblen's work can be examined through his use of the "instinct of workmanship", described as "an assumed human propensity for activity tailored to the efficient achievement of a goal" (Riesman 1953, 51). The instinct of workmanship is vital because it is outlined with a tendency to regard craftsmanship for its own sake. Craftsmanship has no ulterior motives, such as financial gain or self-advancement, but rather a connection to oneself and culture. Workmanship is linked to both Veblen's ideas of "idle curiosity", an interest in the world beyond pragmatic requirements, and "parental bent", the care and interest for the well-being of humanity rather than one's particular kinship. Riesman argued that, "By calling workmanship an instinct, however, Veblen emphasized conscious human purposes less than biological drives, and cultivated purposes less than 'natural' or inherited ones" (Riesman 1953, 52). These cultural frameworks are meant to be used loosely and metaphorically to describe human activity. That is why the charro cowboy tradition, this particular Mexican rural tradition, can be explained through Veblen's discourse.

Veblen's *Instinct of Workmanship and the State of the Industrial Arts* (1914) maintained that the notion of instinct or workmanship was not fixed. He argued of the instinct of workmanship:

> in all their working, the human instincts are …incessantly subject to mutual "contamination," whereby the working of any one is incidentally affected by the bias and proclivities inherent in all the rest; and in so far as these current habits and customs in this way come to reinforce the predispositions comprised under any one instinct or any given group of instincts, the bias so accentuated comes to pervade the habits of thought of all the members of the community and gives a corresponding obliquity to the technological groundwork of the community.
>
> (pp. 40–41)

This contamination of human instincts cannot be entirely explained in biological or psychological terms. On the contrary, this unique cultural assessment in the shift or contamination of human instincts can be examined throughout various socio-cultural contexts, beyond the perspective of the United States. Veblen's examination of the leisure class uncovers how the instinct of workmanship and the parent bent are contaminated by pecuniary achievement and materialism. Ownership becomes a means of visibly achieving a purpose through the accumulation of goods and the instinct of workmanship veers towards celebrating others' pecuniary achievements. Idle curiosity, another of Veblen's brilliant terms referring to the pursuit of knowledge for its own sake, also experiences this form of contamination from economic pressures in an evolving culture. The central argument of this book will examine the contamination of the instinct of workmanship, the parental bent, and the idle curiosity within the context of the Mexican charro cowboy community.

## The Mexican charro cowboy community

While Thorstein Veblen may have been unaware of the existence of the charro cowboy tradition, his cultural theoretical framework is the most fitting to document the changes of this particular rural tradition. The charro cowboy tradition, originating from a complex colonial history, is faced with advancements in technology, rapid urbanization, and industrialization. Although Mexico can be associated with developing characteristics that disqualify it as a powerful and influential country in the Western world, its economic development throughout the last 50 years has led to rapid industrialization and urbanization across all 32 federal entities (Yepes, Pedroni, & Hu 2015). Rural tradition, in any socio-cultural context, experiences change regardless of whether it is voluntary or coerced. The charro tradition is just one of many marginalized cultures in Mexico that has had to culturally adapt to a more modern Mexico that no longer accepts antique customs and rituals outside of their designated national and cultural holidays.

## What is a charro cowboy?

In order to understand how Veblen's cultural and theoretical framework can apply to the charro cowboy, I must first define this complex culture. While the charro cowboy tradition, ultimately known as *la tradición charro* by the majority of Mexicans, has an extensive history, the goal of the following is to provide the reader with a brief, but comprehensive, background of this rural tradition. It is important to acknowledge the history of the charro cowboy tradition because it provides the background of the current changes.

The charro cowboy tradition emerged from a complex and extremely racialized relationship between the Spanish conquistadors and the Mexican indigenous population. During Spanish colonization, Spanish colonial officials attempted to institute strict racial segregation between the indigenous population and the colonizers by implementing the *casta* or caste system, a long-term inherent division in social, economic, and cultural identity that stratified colonial Mexico (Jackson 1999). The Spanish condemned mestizo and indigenous people by denying them resources and rights in colonial society. Indigenous people were granted even fewer rights due to the fact that mestizos became synonymous with bastard offspring leading to a necessary distinction by the Spanish colonizers regarding claims to Spanish ancestry and rights in the *casta* system (De Mente 1996). This condemnation can also be attributed to the pivotal role of Catholicism in the colonization of Mexico. Ultimately, Spanish rule in the 1570s prohibited mestizos and indigenous people from living among one another (Werner 2001).

This forced separation led to creativity among the poor rural lower caste. The *casta* impacted rural life because lower *casta* work was bound with hard labor in small and large haciendas for the benefit of rich Spanish colonizers. According to Carol Merchasin, a scholar of Mexico, "These vast entitlements existed as semi feudal systems, where *patrones* were responsible for the *campesinos*, and the *campesinos* were reciprocally dependent on the *patrones*. Survival tactics for life in this ruthless places, where you could not speak with out permission, were: Don't bring bad news, avoid conflict, don't initiate" (Merchasin 2014). Docility was expected of the mestizo and indigenous groups that worked lengthy and strenuous days. Kathleen Sands, one of the few American scholars of the charro cowboy tradition, stated, "Manpower for herding posed problems for the early cattle and horse breeders of the newly conquered land. Fearful that possession of the horse by natives might threaten Spanish supremacy and well aware that the best physical and psychological weapon they possessed was horsemanship, the Spanish took great care to keep horses out of the hands of the natives..." (Sands 1993, 31). Initially, the *casta* law prohibited mestizos and indigenous people from riding horses or carrying a gun, arising from a fear that accessibility to guns and horses would lead to rebellion by their workers. Nevertheless, this exclusionary practice became disadvantageous to the Spanish hacienda owners because haciendas continued to grow in size, requiring continuous maintenance and labor from the lower *casta* (Meyers 1969; Chevalier 1972; Brading 1978).

Although the first horses were brought to the Americans during the Colombian Exchange in the late 1400s, the horse became an influential source of profit for Mexican haciendas. Horse breeding became a great way to turn a quick profit while the cattle industry grew immensely prior to Mexican independence (Sands 1993).The lower *casta*, faced with more labor, developed their equestrian skills in order to fit the growing demands of the hacienda. Although the Spanish had their own equestrian style and culture, the hacienda workers adapted a saddle style and riding techniques that were unique and significant to them, ultimately forming what is recognized as the modern *charreadas* or charro cowboy events. They adopted the charro cowboy dress and style from the culture of Salamanca, Spain, whose population during the 14th century was predominantly agricultural. According to Robert Smead (2004), charro was a derogatory term in colonial Mexico referring to a peasant worker or a person of lower caste and it was also used as an adjective to describe something in poor taste. Further, Sands (1993) also indicated that the original charro idiom was connected to attire because of the clothing used by 17th-century rural communities. Despite these negative connotations, the charro cowboy became a symbol of resistance and Mexican identity and became exclusively associated with these men. Charro cowboys repurposed this term, unintentionally creating a lasting tradition celebrating positive modes of Mexican rural identity.

The *casta* officially ended on September 16, 1821 when Mexico gained its independence from Spanish rule. Although the *casta* legally distinguished people based on racial classification, social classes became symbolic and were based on socio-economic status. After the *casta*, charro cowboys underwent physical and symbolic discrimination due to their rural origin even though the charro cowboy played a significant role in the defeating Spanish rule. According to James Norman, "In the 1810 War of Independence, which freed Mexico from Spain, the small ranchers and *vaqueros* played a most important part. The war also freed them from Spanish restrictions, and as a result they went to extremes in decorating their costume [with bullets and guns]" (Norman 1970, 85). The horseman became a symbol of power for Mexicans and this symbolism was reflected in art and literature. Yet, the majority of charro cowboys were poor while only a few benefited from Mexico's newly achieved independence. The charro cowboy imagery became synonymous with Mexican patriotism, however, class distinctions within the charro cowboy tradition emerged as newfound opportunities in the accumulation of property became more widely available.

The three-decade presidency of José de la Cruz Porfirio Díaz Mori in the 1870s promoted the rise of economic change in Mexico. Expansion into manufacturing and industry led to the migration of the landless poor into urban spaces (Slatta 1997). According to Sands, "Many of them maintained ties with their villages and sustained an identification with charro traditions as practiced on the haciendas. When charro perfor-mances came to the city, these new factory works were there to swell the audience" (Sands 1993, 61). The presence of the charro cowboy commu-nity in city life gave rise to the use of charro cowboy events as entertain-ment for more than just its participants. Urban spaces were now exposed to this form of entertainment outside the bounds of hacienda life. The charro cowboy tradition became a pastime in urban Mexico, leading to cultural shifts within the charro cowboy community. Class distinctions, not just in the charro cowboy community, exacerbated the tension between revolutionaries and Porfirio Díaz's political followers.

Upper class Mexican used the charro cowboy tradition as a method to elevate their class status by distinguishing themselves by dress, speech, expensive horses, etc. For example, they could afford the most expensive charro cowboy gala out-fits, often threaded in gold and silver. By the end of the 18th and early 19th cen-turies, there were evident class distinctions within the charro cowboy community that stemmed from Mexico's changing economic structure (Wilkie and Michaels 1969). The wealthiest charro cowboys could afford to invest money, making it possible for the charro cowboy tradition to become a source of entertainment for Mexicans. As Mexico's economic structure depended more on industry rather than agriculture, the charro cowboy tradition became a symbol rather than a rural lifestyle. Sands (1993) stated:

> Although the traditional haciendas disappeared, the charro who had survived the war and could find vaquero work or revive their small independent ranchero operations returned to take up familiar roles. Even village celebrations and rodeos were revived, so charros could show off their skills as they had done for centuries. But for those who went to the city, and even those that remained in the countryside, only memories of the old way of life on haciendas remained. Charro shows had been discontinued during the war, and although horses continued to be a major form of transportation for rural people, horsemanship was not a necessity for the city dweller. For many Mexicans, particularly for the vaqueros, hacendados, and hacienda administrators who migrated to the cities, and for their offspring, the possibility of losing the horse-manship skills that had linked charro so closely to the evolution of national identity was a frightening prospect.
>
> (p. 73)

While economic growth in the late 1800s benefited Mexican political adversaries, economic development was also experienced by few wealthy estate owners—recognized as rancheros—who owned hacendados or large plots of land and were able to acquire large portions of land leading to many rural vaqueros, hacendados, and charro cowboys migrating into Mexican cities for work and with the desire to preserve their charro cowboy culture.

The tension between the lower class and upper class Mexicans led to the Mexican Revolution in 1910, ousting Porfirio Díaz from political power. The horse once again played an important role for the revolutionaries in the defeat of Porfirio Díaz's regime (Griffith and Fernández 1988). Important figures such as Pancho Villa and Emiliano Zapata became famous public figures of the Revolution as well in the charro cowboy community. In particular, Emiliano Zapata and other vaqueros that fought in the revolution had ties to the charro cowboy community. Zapata grew up with the charro cowboy tradition and his family experienced financial hardship due to Porfirio Díaz's policies. Emiliano Zapata dressed in the charro style and was often characterized as the charro of charros (Newell 1979). Zapata is such a symbol of charro cowboy tradition that many modern charro cowboys still refer to him as a charro that they admire. As Zapata gained popularity and leadership in the revolution against Porfirio Díaz, revolutionaries were associated with the charro cowboy community. Sands stated, "[Zapata was characterized as] the perfect charro, a man who espoused democratic principles, rose from and remained loyal to the oppressed, displayed the highest level of equestrian skill, led the army of the south in the cause of justice, and was assassinated by a corrupt government. Even his assassination contributes to his charro reputation" (Sands 1993, 71). The Mexican Revolution officially ended in 1920, yet the charro cowboy symbolism was re-established as a matter of national importance representing all levels of society.

The charro cowboy community remained active in the rural margins of Mexico. However, a governmental push to preserve Mexico's national traditions and customs prompted the formal organization of the National Association of Charros in 1919 in Mexico City. The National Association of Charros was organized to preserve the charro cowboy tradition in Mexico City and led to formal organization of charro cowboys from other states such as Jalisco, Hidalgo, and Guanajuato. Further, the Mexican government in 1933 announced that the charro tradition was the national sport of Mexico and funded the *Federación Mexicana de la Charrería* (Mexican Federation of Charro Cowboys). This action reaffirmed official attempts to preserve the elements of the charro cowboy community's traditions and customs. According to an interview I conducted with the *Museo de la Charrería* (Museum of Charro Cowboys) in 2014, their collection houses artifacts such as the original saddle of Pancho Villa and also serves as the ceremonial meeting place for the Mexican Federation of Charro Cowboys.

The importance of the Mexican Federation of Charro Cowboys is worth noting, as I will reference the influence of that powerful organization throughout this book. The formal formation of this organization demonstrates the slow shift in the original intentions of the charro cowboy community, creativity in defiance of marginalization. The Mexican Federation of Charro Cowboys controls the regional and national competitions or *charreadas* across Mexico (Franco 1990). In 1934, President Abelardo L. Rodríguez instituted the *Día Nacional del Charro* or the National Day of the Charro on September 14 two days before Mexico's Independence Day solidifying the charro cowboy's national identity (Carreño King 2000). Every year, on September 14, Mexico celebrates the symbolism of the charro cowboy and in 2011 many self-identified charro cowboys were invited to celebrate at the epicenter of Mexico City, El Zócalo (home of the National Palace, an official presidential space).

The formal institutionalization of the charro cowboy tradition reaffirmed the respected position of the charro cowboy as a national and cultural symbol of Mexico. Mexican popular culture used the charro cowboy character in their films and songs to characterize a national sentiment and symbolism of the rural lifestyle. Olga Nájera-Ramirez (1994), an anthropologist specializing in folklore, argued:

> Like other cultural groups Mexicans have been engaged in constructing and displaying images of their culture groups consumption for a long time... The popular 1940s Mexican song of my epigraph proclaims the charro, the dashing Mexican horseman, as the pride of Mexico... The charro figures prominently in a variety of discourses including, but not limited to, film, music, folkloric dance, and literature.
>
> (p. 1)

It was no surprise that in the same decade that the charro cowboy tradition gained institutional legitimacy, Mexican popular culture was dominated by charro cowboy imagery. Similar to the importance of the Western American cowboy, the epitome of Mexican masculinity and identity was deeply rooted in the charro cowboy performance. Significantly, the use of the charro cowboy in film and music portrayed how people from rural communities coped with the Mexico's rapid urbanization and social class issues unique to Mexican society.

The personification of the charro cowboy became generalized and reduced to stereotypes regarding their womanizing, drinking habits, and passion for dignity and respect. The American western film genre in the United States gained popularity after the charro cowboy had already become a well-established figure in Mexican cinema and borrowed from the charro cowboy imagery (Allen 1998). The American cowboy gained more popularity than the Mexican charro cowboy because of notion of Manifest Destiny that held Americans as exceptional and endowed with God's approval.[1] D.H. Figueredo stated, "This message was popularized in movies and novels and comic books. So widely accepted was the notion that by the early 20th century, cowboy was a word commonly known and used in many languages, while vaquero was only recognized and uttered in Spanish" (Figueredo, 2014, 8). While the cowboy is universally recognized, the charro cowboy is only recognized by residents of

Central and South America. This further exemplifies how Mexico and other Latin American cultures are marginalized because they are seen as being developing countries.

Today the charro cowboy community exists on both sides of the Mexican border. The modern charro cowboy refers to the embodiment of a particular type of culture, etiquette, mannerism, clothing, tradition, and social status that is linked to its complex historical past (Nájera-Ramírez 1994; Marquez 2016, 2018). The image of a charro cowboy as a popular cultural figure has been reduced to mariachi music and antiquated modes of life. While the charro cowboy is celebrated and remembered, the reduction of its imagery has created a disconnect between the charro cowboy community and the greater Mexican population. The charro cowboy's original connection to Mexican nationalism and patriotism are only rekindled during Mexico's commemoration of the past or blatant expressions of Mexican rural identity. The charro cowboy is no longer the dominant figure in popular culture or even the rural or urban way of life (Marquez 2018). Many urban Mexicans are unfamiliar with the presence of the charro cowboy community or that *charreadas* or events occur within their surrounding communities. Mexicans can easily recognize elements of the charro cowboy figure, such as the sombrero, but are no longer familiar with their modes of life or their subculture.

The charro cowboy community survives through active participation in formal and informal *charreadas* throughout Mexico. Without continuous active participation in the charro cowboy community, the charro cowboy tradition would not survive. Entry into the charro cowboy community is generally passed down from one charro family to another; however, the skills, customs, and beliefs of the charro cowboy community can be acquired from interested outsiders who wish to compete or marry into the community. Interested outsiders can acclimatize, however, and their journey within the community frequently encounters abuse and rejection. Distinctions within the charro cowboy community are continuously formed and they present an important element in the proclivity to separate authentic members from perceived imposters.

Men and women in the charro cowboy community undergo a particular type of socialization into the charro cowboy tradition, whether from birth or adulthood. The charro cowboy community, under the guidance and authority of the Mexican Federation of Charros, is aware of the fact that they are now a marginal culture rather than the dominant narrative in Mexico. Although the charro cowboy community has remained the same in many ways, it is not completely impervious to external changes in Mexican society. This book will analyse how modernity transforms or effects rural cultural traditions like the charro tradition and how rural cultural traditions continue to stay alive, despite the presence of dominant sport cultures like Mexican soccer. Further, I will examine how members of the charro cowboy community produce, maintain, and enact the charro cowboy tradition.

This book will apply Veblen's theories to this particular Mexican equestrian culture, dating back to colonial Mexico, to best assess its changes and the contamination of its original beliefs and customs. Veblen's combination of idle curiosity, parental bent, and instinct of workmanship describe the original intention of the charro cowboy community's informal organization. Further, his argument regarding the peaceable and the barbaric, the identifiable contrast separating those with motives to continue tradition for its own sake from those with motives to exploit it for honor or money, are relevant to the rising implications of the accumulation of wealth within the charro cowboy community. Idle curiosity entails no vested interest and no waste to humanity while gaining "something for nothing" is an emerging predatory theme in the charro cowboy community. As the charro cowboy community becomes more exposed to business principles, the push for pecuniary interests become more critical than cultural performance and preservation.

## Methodological approach

As I established earlier, this book uses an ethnographic case study, the charro cowboy community, to show the importance of Thorstein Veblen's theories in understanding qualitative and cultural work in sociology. The following chapters will provide only a snapshot of the very complex culture of the charro cowboy community in Mexico, however, these findings demonstrate how subtle changes in rural culture can have a significant impact on the people who work hard to maintain, reproduce, and enact these traditions. It is significant to my use of Thorstein Veblen to explain my methodological approach in order to understand why his theoretical interpretation is the most valuable in making sense of this Mexican rural tradition.

Similar to Veblen, I began this project by drawing from my own life experiences as the granddaughter of a generational charro cowboy, unfamiliar with the significance of my own Mexican roots. My family immigrated to the United States in the early 1990s with only a suitcase, fearful of our surroundings and only having our culture to rely on. Although I was raised in rural New York State, my mother told me tales of my grandfather and his small ranch outside of Mexico City. She referred me to the three generational legacy of charro cowboys that had become part of my family identity and culture. I was intrigued by the rich culture of charro cowboy tradition that had had an impact in my upbringing. My mother had always told me that our family was different from other Mexican families, but I did not have another frame of reference to compare until I talked to other Mexican immigrant families from Mexico City who did not share my family history. They were often confused with my family's very conservative customs and beliefs. Although there was a consensus of machismo and racism among my Mexican friends, I began to realize that my charro cowboy history played an important role in the manner in which my family synthesized issues of gender, class, and race.

In 2012, I had the honor of meeting my great grandfather before he passed at the age of 91 in the small village where he spent his life with his wife and raised his 12 children. This experience inspired me to focus my graduate research on the charro cowboy tradition that regulates the life of so many of my family members. I had so many questions about the perceptions, worldviews, and life outcomes of those who actively participated in the charro cowboy community, focusing on how they dealt with a country no longer romanticized by rancho living. The charro cowboy tradition impacted my own mother's life outcomes as she was denied access to high school because she was a woman. My grandfather believed that women should not have too much education since their primary goal was to get married and have children. Once my mother reached puberty, my grandfather stopped taking to her school and no one in my family fought to allow my mother to continue her education, not even my grandmother. At first glance, I thought this was unique to my mother's experience in the late 1970s, but I then discovered that my first cousin from my generation was also denied access to education.

Mexico, as a country, has continued to transform as it has become more urbanized and industrialized in the last few decades. Although the Mexican charro cowboy carries a great deal of historical significance and nationalist symbolism, many (both American and Mexican) do not know about its operation and function in contemporary society. The charro cowboy tradition, in this study, should be understood as a process in which individuals reproduce, maintain, and enact this particular subset of rural Mexican customs. From this point forward, the generalizations I make about the charro cowboy tradition come from the empirical data collected.

In order to address my research questions regarding the charro cowboy community, I conducted an in-depth participatory ethnographic analysis during the summer months (May to August) of 2012–2015. Using my personal access to the charro cowboy community (my maternal family members as gatekeepers), I conducted research in six different states in Mexico: Mexico, Jalisco, Guanajuato, Aguascalientes, Hidalgo, and Puebla. Throughout my first year of my ethnographic analysis, I befriended a charro cowboy rookie (a charro cowboy without any generational ties) (Miguel[2]) from a mid-level team who acted as my supplementary gatekeeper to the experiences of charro cowboy rookies. Gatekeepers play a crucial role in social research methods because they are usually the researcher's initial contact and access to participants (McGivern 2006; May 2011; Crowhurst 2013). Although I have an access point, my researcher status labeled me an outsider to the charro cowboy community. Miguel was able to identify crucial contradictions of the charro cowboy tradition that had not been identified by others with generational ties (more than one generational tie to the charro cowboy tradition). He was able to recruit other charro cowboy rookies to trust me and my research project.

My last name was well recognized in Mexico because of my family's charro cowboy reputation, resulting in open doors for my research. Because many charro cowboys associated me with my actively competing family members, they treated me as if I was part of the community, therefore expecting me to behave within the bounds of my age and gender. Since I was raised in the United States, many charro cowboys were eager to teach the "ways of my people" and excused my behavior when I did not fulfill social expectations of charro women. My unique position as an outsider and insider presented many opportunities that were not necessarily afforded to other researchers of the charro cowboy community. This is because many charro cowboys tried to protect me from being mistaken as an outsider and made sure to vouch for my work to other potential research participants. I developed close research relationships with an additional ten charro cowboy men and women throughout my three years in the charro cowboy community that required follow-up questioning throughout my ethnographic research. However, I interviewed and observed a total of 72 people during my time in Mexico. My respondent's ages ranged from 18 to 78 years old. In the three years I conducted interviews and qualitative observations, I shadowed the experiences of both generational and non-generational charro cowboys in national, regional, and friendly tournaments throughout central Mexico.

Using a symbolic interactionist approach, I was able to examine how indigenous status, class, and gender were uniquely negotiated among charro cowboys who did not believe there were any forms of inequality or discrimination present in the charro cowboy tradition. Matters of indigenous status, class, and gender were shaped by social context and patterns in the interactions between members in the charro cowboy community. Drawing from the qualitative work on race, class, and gender that examines the what an individual "does" rather than what an individual "has", I evaluated the different dimensions of variation within the charro cowboy community that stratified legitimacy (Best 2003; Bettie 2003; Moore 2002; West and Fenstermaker 1991). The use of language, in particular the use of charro cowboy slang, is the quickest identifier of outsiders, usually breaking into the charro cowboy community as adults rather than socialized as children. The examination of how respondents constructed their identity was crucial for how charro cowboys cope with the gradual changes of the charro cowboy tradition. Veblen's scholarship helps distinguish these gradual changes, in particular the evolution of the charro cowboy's instinct of workmanship.

Since this research was an in-depth participatory observation ethnography, I worked alongside charro cowboys from various backgrounds. In the months of May 2013 to August 2013, I traveled with a midlevel team (they were professional but not prestigious) and lived with the family on the ranch. I took care of their children when necessary, helped with the cleaning and cooking, and helped with the horses. As a researcher, I would ride alongside them learning the specifics of the charro cowboy tradition while I would watch them work. This was important to determine patterns and normal daily activities of my participants.

During the months of May 2014 to August 2014, I lived with a divorced charro woman and her two children. In this small amount of time, I was able to learn even more about the valuable notions of decency and respectability that is required of all generational women while documenting how nonconforming individuals face stigma and discrimination from the charro cowboy community. In addition, I traveled to different parts of central Mexico in order to gain more access to the wealthier side of the charro cowboy community, group of charro cowboys echoing Veblen's perception of a leisure class structure. In the last portion of my ethnography (May 2015 to August 2015), I was able to do follow ups of my interviews and work with a team of elite charro cowboys, highly regarded throughout the community and often treated as celebrities among their peers. The summer months were crucial to my analysis since the majority of important competitions take place during this time. It was important to my analysis to have my observation settings vary from competition arenas to family homes in order to better assess the charro cowboy culture.

In my interviews, I asked questions about their beliefs regarding the charro cowboy tradition, brotherhood, relationships, team support, employment, newcomers, expenses, etc. The questions were open-ended to encourage discussion about the charro cowboy tradition and concerns that respondents may have had in their life at the time. However, I did ask standard demographic question such as age, education status, employment, and socio-economic status. These interviews lasted from 15 minutes to two hours, depending on the availability of the respondent. Interviews were recorded using an audio recording device and were later transcribed in Spanish to be translated in English. Observations were recorded in a notebook and 300 pages were recorded during my time in Mexico. Respondents were informed about their rights as participants, as stipulated by the Institutional Review Board. Transcriptions and observations were later coded using qualitative data analysis and research software, Atlas.ti.

As a female ethnographer of the charro cowboy community, charro cowboy men often thought of me as potential love interest (see Chapter 3 for further details). This made interviewing and observations accessible, but many charro cowboys often did not respect the boundaries of a researcher and respondent. Interviews where charro cowboy men were drunk were usually really difficult as these men did not respect personal space or boundaries. I found that this was true for all charro cowboy men of various ages and socio-economic backgrounds. In addition, charro cowboy women with boyfriends and husbands initially mistook me as a threat to their relationships because many had not met a female researcher or were highly suspicious of my intentions. This presented a unique opportunity to analyse how charro cowboy women treat or rather mistreat female outsiders or women who violate the norms of respectability. I had to censor my own identity as a Mexican-American lesbian and conform to the standards of charro cowboy femininity and respectability in order to avoid any potential issues.

An ethnographic analysis was better suited for the analysis of culture and identity formation due to the significance of the narratives and actions of the people actively participating in the charro cowboy tradition. The intersectional analysis of race, class, and gender would have been impossible without this methodology as many members of the charro cowboy tradition were resistant to outsiders. I concentrated my analysis on uncovering not only the way in which the charro cowboy tradition has changed, but also how it has remained the same despite a number of varying external factors. The following chapters will intentionally apply the work of Thorstein Veblen to make sense of this extensive ethnographic work and demonstrate the utility of Veblen's theoretical approach as advantageous to ethnographers of culture.

## Notes

1 Although the American cowboy is portrayed in American film as white, the earliest American cowboys were in fact not white, but Mexican, black, and Native American (Homann 2006).
2 The names of the interview participants were changed to protect their privacy.

## References

Allen, Michael, *Rodeo Cowboys in the North American Imagination*. Reno: University of Nevada Press. 1998.

Best, Amy L., "Doing Race in the Context of Feminist Interviewing: Constructing Whiteness through Talk." *Qualitative Inquiry*, vol. 9 (2003): 895–914.

Bettie, Julie, *Women without Class: Girls, Race, and Identity*. Berkeley: University of California Press. 2003.

Brading, David A., *Haciendas and ranchos in the Mexican bajio*. Cambridge: Cambridge University Press. 1978.

Carreño King, Tania. "Yo soy mexicano, mi tierra es bravía." *Artes de México*, no. 50 (2000): 50–61.

Chevalier, Francois, *Land and society in colonial Mexico: The great hacienda*. Berkeley: University of California Press. 1972.

Crowhurst, Isabel, "The fallacy of the instrumental gate? Contextualising the process of gaining access through gatekeepers." *International Journal of Social Research Methodology: Theory & Practice*, vol. 16, no 6 (May 2013): 463–475.

De Mente, Boye, *NTC's Dictionary of Mexican Cultural Code Word: The Complete Guide to Key Woords That Express How the Mexicans Think, Communicate, and Behave*. New York: McGraw-Hill Education. 1996.

Diggins, John P., *Thorstein Veblen: Theorist of the Leisure Class*. Princeton: Princeton University Press. 1999.

Dorfman, Joseph. *Thorstein Veblen and His America*. New York: Augustus M Kelly Pubs. 1934.

Figueredo, D.H., *Revolvers and Pistolas, Vaqueros and Caballeros: Debunking the Old West*. Santa Barbara, California: ABC-CLIO. 2014.

Franco, María Elena. "Charrería, Recurso Turístico de México." Master's thesis, School of Tourism, Autonomous University of Nayarit, Mexico, 1990.

Griffith, James S. and Celestino Fernández. "Mexican Horse Races and Cultural Values: The Case of Los Corridos del Merino." *Western Folklore, vol.* 47, no. 2 (April 1988): 129–151.

Homann, Ronnie D. "Contemporary Cowboy Culture and the Rise of American Postmodern Solidarity." Dissertation thesis, Department of Sociology, Texas A&M University, 2006.

Jackson, Robert H., *Race, Caste, and Status: Indians in Colonial Spanish America.* Albuquerque: University of New Mexico Press. 1999.

Marquez, Beatriz A., "The Effects of Hacienda Culture on the Gendered Division of Labor within the Charro Community." *Gender Issues* (2016): 1–20.

Marquez, Beatriz A., "Shift in Social Character: Charro Cultural Representations in Mexican Popular Culture." *Studies in Latin American Popular Culture* (2018): 30–46.

May, Tim, *Social Research Issues, Methods and Process.* Maidenhead: Open University Press. 2011.

McGivern, Yvonne., *The practice of market and social research: An introduction.* Harlow: Financial Times. Prentice Hall. 2006.

Merchasin, Carol, *How it Goes in Mexico: Essays from an expatriate.* New York: Shebooks. 2014.

Mestrovic, Stjepan, *Thorstein Veblen on Culture and Society.* London: Sage Publications. 2003.

Meyers, Sandra, *The Ranch in Spanish Texas, 1691–1800.* El Paso: Texas Western Press. University of Texas. 1969.

Moore, Valerie A. , "The Collaborative Emergence of Race in Children's Play: A Case Study of Two Summer Camps." *Social Problems*, vol. 49 (2002): 58–78.

Nájera-Ramírez, Olga, *Engendering Nationalism: Identity, Discourse and the Mexican Charro.* Santa Cruz, CA: Chicano/Latino Research Center. 1994.

Newell, Peter E. *Zapata de Mexico.* Somerville, Mass.: Black Thorn Books. 1979.

Norman, James, *Charro: Mexican Horseman.* Austin: University of Texas Press. 1970.

Plotkin, Sidney. *The Anthem Companion to Thorstein Veblen.* New York: Anthem Press. 2017.

Riesman, David. *Thorstein Veblen.* New York: Charles Scribner's Sons. 1953.

Sands, Kathleen M., *Charrería Mexicana: An Equestrian Folk Tradition.* Tucson: University of Arizona Press. 1993.

Slatta, Richard W., *Comparing Cowboys and Frontiers.* Norman: University of Oklahoma. 1997.

Smead, Robert N., *Vocabulario Vaquero/ Cowboy Talk: A Dictionary of Spanish Terms from the American West.* Norman, Oklahoma: University of Oklahoma Press. 2004.

Veblen, Thorstein. "The Barbarian Status of Women." *American Journal of Sociology*, vol. 4, no. 4 (1899): 503–514

Veblen, Thorstein. *The Instinct of Workmanship, and the State of the Industrial Arts.* New ed. New York: A.M. Kelley, Bookseller. 1964[1914].

Veblen, Thorstein. *On the Nature and Uses of Sabotage.* New York: Dial Publishing Company, 1919, reprint, New York: Oriole Editions, 1971.

Veblen, Thorstein. *The Theory of Business Enterprise 1904.* New York: A.M. Kelley, Bookseller. 1965[1904].

Veblen, Thorstein. *The Theory of the Leisure Class: An Economic Study of Institutions.* New York: Reprint by The New American Library, 1953[1889].

Veblen, Thorstein. *The Vested Interest and the Common Man.* Reprint by New York: Augustus M. Kelley Pubs. 1963[1920].

Werner, Michael S., ed., *Concise Encyclopedia of Mexico.* London: Fitzroy Dearborn. 2001.

West, Candace, and Sarah Fenstermaker. "Doing Difference." *Gender and Society*, vol. 9 (1991): 8–37.

Wilkie, James W. and Albert L. Michaels. *Revolution in Mexico: Years of Upheaval, 1910–1940*. New York: Knopf. 1969.

Yepes, Conceptión V., Peter L. Pedroni, and Xingwei Hu. *Crimes and the Economy in Mexican States: Heterogeneous Panel Estimates (1993–2012)*. Washington, D.C.: International Monetary Fund. 2015.

# 2 The influence of business principles

The charro cowboy tradition, originally, was unorganized, informal, and most importantly, spontaneous. The men who worked on the large haciendas during the colonial and post-colonial rural areas of Mexico were focused on creating a legitimate space for their horsemanship skills, separate from Spanish domination. The original function of the charro cowboy community was to create a safe space to demonstrate marginalized charro cowboy horsemanship skills while—what Veblen would have called the instinct of workmanship—providing an opportunity to form bonds with other charro cowboys in their community. The charro cowboy tradition, as I have previously mentioned, emerged as a rural counterculture that stressed the freedom to roam the land and to express the charro cowboy identity. The golden age of Mexican cinema romanticized rural living and the charro cowboy identity, but marginal small towns in rural Mexico very much relied on the charro cowboy community for more than just substance. Rural villages throughout Mexico used the charro cowboy tradition for entertainment and celebrations that incorporated, not surprisingly, Catholic symbols such as the Virgin Mary, Jesus, and regional saints into their team names and arenas. The charro cowboy community was a source of pride in many pueblos and these events were often the only form of inter-pueblo interactions, allowing for romantic relationships to blossom. Friendly competition between pueblos was common and was often not formally organized. It was not at all uncommon for *charreadas*, or charro cowboy competitions, to spring up spontaneously.

*Charreadas* were not about winning or about pecuniary gain, but rather enjoying the company of other members of the charro cowboy community. The original *charreadas* were usually between adjacent pueblos and these informal events had no judges, no time limits, and no pressure to win. Teams usually comprised two or three families with access to horses and land. Older generations of charro cowboys and their spectators still remember the lengthy *charreadas* and the lack of organization during these festivities. Many of the older community members recall lengthy *charreadas* that might last for hours. *Charreadas* resembled family gatherings with food, copious tequila, and cigars for the men. There was live music for spectators to dance to and the *lienzos* or arenas were open to the public free of charge. But since the formal establishment of the charro cowboy tradition as the official sport of Mexico in 1933, the Mexican Federation of Charros has slowly implemented formal regulation of the charro cowboy rodeo events or *las suertes charras*. [1] Further, the Mexican Federation of Charros unified various regional associations in order to establish a concrete order of *charreadas* throughout Mexico. Since 1933, the Mexican Federation of Charros has supervised the majority of the *charreadas* and charro cowboy associations in the country, essentially controlling what is and is not allowed during competitions. This standardization has caused great strain amongst the charro cowboy community.

The Mexican Federation of Charros functions as the gatekeeper and protector of the rules and regulations that make a *charreadas* a legitimate charro cowboy event. Their headquarters are located in the heart of Mexico City. Even the *lienzos* in which charro cowboys compete are liable to strict specifications and measurements. For example, according the Mexican Federation of Charros's *Reglamento Oficial General Para Competencias* (Official and General Rules for Competitions 2012–2016), *lienzos* must measure 60 meters long by 12 meters wide and have an arena that should be 40 meters in diameter. *Charreadas* must also be classified as official or friendly prior to the date of competition, leaving very little opportunity for spontaneity. Charro cowboy teams must register their *charreadas* with the Mexican Federation of Charros in order to use their judges or rules and pay dues to maintain their membership. This is only one example of how much control the Mexican Federation of Charros has upon those who wish to compete in the charro cowboy community. Charro cowboys do not have much agency to stray outside of the bounds of the Official and General Rules for Competitions. Either they follow regulations or face disqualification.

Due to a growing pressure to turn the Mexican Federation of Charros and the various associations into functional and profit-producing businesses, charro cowboy competitions have become more standardized. Standardization, as we understand it in capitalism, leaves very room for creativity, leading products to be identical to one another. In this chapter, I utilize Veblen's *Theory of Business Enterprise* (1904) and *Theory of the Leisure Class* (1899) to highlight the collision between the business enterprise and the machine process in producing standardization, fungibility, and the pursuit of pecuniary gain. Although Veblen's original analysis focused on industrialization of American life, a similar analysis can be made in the context of Mexican charro cowboys experiencing pressure to conform to business principles. I will demonstrate how this standardization chips away elements of the charro cowboy tradition, ultimately changing its intrinsic nature. I argue that these business principles have an expanding impact on the class divisions with the charro cowboy community. In particular, charro cowboy business principles provide the opportunity for the emergence of a charro cowboy leisure class more focused on winning and making money than upholding the original traditions.

## Applying Veblen's theories

The increased power of the Mexican Federation of Charros has filtered into other aspects of the charro cowboy community. In particular, charro cowboy teams are now managed by charro cowboy *jefes* (bosses) and organizers. The charro cowboy *jefes* and organizers serve the purpose of further regulating the creativity of the competing charro cowboy and profiting from a team's success. Charro cowboy *jefes* are the owners and financial endorsers of particular charro cowboy teams throughout Mexico, operating more like absentee owners rather than active participants. Although Ramírez Barreto (2009) referred to these charro cowboy *jefes* as *paganinis*, I choose to employ the term most frequently used by charro cowboys that I interviewed during this ethnography. This management of charro cowboy teams is a relatively new development in the last 50 years, but it has become a common practice among the more notable and prestigious teams. There seems to be a bureaucratic push by the Mexican Federation of Charros to operate the charro cowboy traditions and community like professional athletic teams in order generate more revenue and corporate sponsorship. The organizers I spoke to throughout my research frequently mentioned their desire to make *charreadas* into national events televised throughout Mexico, similar to soccer games. However, the charro cowboy community has yet to reach this goal. *Charreadas* now place more emphasis on opportunities to expand business rather than reproducing the charro cowboy culture. Standardization, quantitative precision, physical requirements, equipment uniformity, and other manifestations of what Veblen called "business principles" ensure that charro cowboys fall into line and submit to the Mexican Federation of Charros.

The elements of the charro cowboy tradition are both peaceable and barbaric, but in the last two decades, the community has incorporated more barbaric principles. In Veblen's *Theory of the Leisure Class* (1899), the traits of a peaceable society have no notions of status, distinctions between gender roles, and no individual ownership as the dominant feature of their society. Emphasis is placed on the instinct of workmanship, idle curiosity, and parental bent to serve humanity beyond the direction of pragmatism and vested interests. Veblen states, "...in all their working, the human instincts are...incessantly subject to mutual 'contamination,' whereby the working of anyone is affected by the bias and proclivities inherent in all the rest" (Veblen 1920, 40). This contamination refers to how peaceable traits do not remain unchanged, but are subject to the shifts in the dominant culture. Idle curiosity is defined as a peaceable characteristic due to its "non-directed activity of exploration in the search for answers to life interests" in which "play" is at the center (O'Hara 1993). Contamination of an individual's idle curiosity occurs when there is a vested interest that directs a person to pecuniary gain or social status. The inclusion of vested interests in peaceable traits fundamentally transforms the actor's relationship with their culture.

Barbaric culture, where exploitative and predatory characteristics are dominant, places great emphasis on the leisure class rather than individuals who perform manual labor, industry work, or anything associated with everyday survival. Barbaric characteristics emerge, not solely due to later stages of societal development, but rather through slow transitional changes to cultural habits. Veblen clearly laid out two conditions whereby society could go from peaceable to barbaric. He stated:

> The conditions apparently necessary to its emergence in a consistent form are: (1) the community must be of a predatory habit of life (war or the hunting of large game or both); that is to say, the men, who constitute the inchoate leisure class in these cases must be habituated in the infliction of injury by force and stratagem; (2) subsistence must be obtainable on sufficiently easy terms to admit of the exemption of a considerable portion of the community from steady application to a routine of labour.
>
> (Veblen 1899, 5)

Barbarism, unlike peaceable society, stratifies employment by creating distinctions based on honor and prestige. Peaceable occupations that contribute to society without the motivation of pecuniary gain are often categorized as unworthy and unimportant. Social classes with the contamination of the predatory habit of life excel in society, not because they work harder or make more money, but because they exhibit a vested interest in exploitation of others. The peaceful worker is replaced with the businessman, motivated by pecuniary gain and the accumulation of wealth.

Vested interest in the instinct of workmanship may lead to exploitation and chicanery in the pursuit of status, honor, and prestige. Similar to peaceable dominant societies, barbaric characteristics still employ the instinct of workmanship, idle curiosity, and parental bent, nevertheless the aspects of barbaric culture or characteristics based in exploitation and self-interest change what is considered worthy. In a barbaric and predatory culture, a worker that does not have vested interest and exploitive means is considered to be unworthy by the dominant society at large. Veblen argued, "Those employments which are to be classes as exploit are worthy, honorable, noble; other employments, which do not contain this element of exploitation, and especially those which imply subservience or submission, are unworthy, debasing, ignorable" (Veblen 1899, 8). The work of women and lower ranking men is deemed less honorable than that of able-bodied men. Aside from social class distinctions, gendered characteristics can also expose bias of barbaric and predatory habits.

The gendered and social distinctions are detectable in the charro cowboy community when examining how women and lower ranking men are treated and talked about casually. I will explore this further in Chapter 5. This chapter will explore how business principles have permeated into the very cultural fabric of the charro cowboy community. Despite the fact that the charro community is by no means a "purely" peaceable tradition, the emergence of the power of business principles has made the newer generation of charro cowboy participants more barbaric and predatory than previous generations.

Veblen argued that no society reflects truly one particular cultural habit, that is, no society can exhibit only barbaric or predatory habits. Barbaric and peaceable habits exist together but not proportionate to one another, and are often dependent on the evolution of society. The presence of business principles shifts the emphasis of cultural habits to the barbaric and predatory, while peaceable habits are not removed but suppressed.

The charro cowboy tradition had little industrial innovation, meaning that the fundamental elements rely on horsemanship skills. Nevertheless, business principles have gradually become more valuable among wealthier charro cowboys, specifically those individuals who can finance entire charro cowboy teams. There is power and money to be gained for the business minded charro cowboy. Veblen argued, "The business man, especially the business man of wide and authoritative discretion, has become a controlling force in industry, because, through the mechanism of investments and markets, he controls the plants and processes, and these set the pace and determine the direction of movement for the rest" (Veblen 1904, 40). Although Veblen was referring to industrial activity, his description of the businessman is useful in assessing charro cowboys with more prominent barbaric and predatory cultural habits that exploit the tradition.

As mentioned earlier, the charro cowboy community commenced from Spanish condemnation of mestizo and indigenous work. Mestizo and indigenous workers of the colonial period were defined as inferior by law and thus, their work was regarded as unworthy. The charro cowboy tradition of the colonial period had peaceable elements because they had a function in rural society and there was no incentive to profit. It was idle curiosity that allowed the early charro cowboys to shape their equestrian skills into what they are today. Although there are some aspects of barbaric culture in the early charro cowboy tradition (i.e. the domination of animals and discriminatory practices against women and lower ranking men), the early charro cowboy's barbaric and predatory habits were not heavily influenced by business principles. They were not particularly interested in business because they were part of the inferior class, holding no financial power in society. As the charro cowboy gained popularity among the leisure class due to its national iconography, upper class Mexicans were able to use the charro cowboy tradition as a method of elevating their status and prestige. For example, charro cowboy *jefes* often do not participate in *charreadas* but benefit from the success of the work of others. Charro cowboy *jefes* are able to display wealth through their disposable incomes and status while their employees perform the hard labor.

Before its cultural institutionalization and established legitimacy from the Mexican government, charro cowboys participated in *charreadas* for the sole purpose of enacting their culture. There was no need for charro cowboy *jefes* because multiple generations of family members comprised the charro cowboy team and managed their own horses and equipment. Winning or losing was not the objective of the *charreadas* but rather *charreadas* were essential for the reproduction and enactment of the charro cowboy culture. Veblen stated, "Industry is effort that goes to create a new thing, with a new purpose given it by the fashioning hand of its maker out of passive ('brute') material: while exploit, so far as it results in an outcome useful to the agent, is the conversion to his own ends of energies previously directed to some other end by another agent" (Veblen 1889, 7). The charro cowboy community has many components of exploitation that affect gender relations, class, and racial category that have been exacerbated by predatory culture. In the case of the charro cowboy *jefe*, exploitation of others produces money and prestige that is not shared with others. The emerging role of the charro cowboy *jefes* is just one form of the way in which the charro cowboy community has been altered by predatory and barbaric culture.

Veblen does not consider the business enterprise and the machine process to be a solely barbaric characteristic. Both have peaceable origins such as the instinct of workmanship, idle curiosity, and parental bent, yet business' barbaric characteristics allows for peaceable qualities to be suppressed. Veblen stated, "The margin of admissible variation, in time, place, form, and amount is narrowed" (Veblen 1904, 4). As mentioned previously, the charro cowboy competition was open-ended and spontaneous. Today, spontaneity is no longer the norm in the charro cowboy community because *charreadas* are now timed, organized, regulated, and have judges appointed and certified by the Mexican Federation of Charros. *Charreadas* are also ranked and some are considered to be more legitimate than others. For example, only men can be judges for competitions and they serve as "the maximum authority in competitions" according to the Official and General Rules for Competitions 2012–2016. In addition to a judge, a *caporal* or an impartial charro cowboy moderator is required to supervise *charreadas* to ensure the timely operation of the charro cowboy teams because competitions are now subjected to time restrictions. Before this, *charreadas* events could take several hours to complete. The *caporal* is not a judge but another method of securing standardization within the tradition.

The freedom of the charro cowboy to express their tradition has become more restricted thus suppressing peaceable idle curiosity. Idle curiosity, in the context of the charro cowboy community, pertains to the lack of exploitation and emphasis on discovery. Further, the instinct of workmanship also becomes contaminated in predatory culture due to the restrictions of standardization and regulation. The consequences of this standardization can be understood more clearly when Veblen stated, "In any community where such an invidious comparison of persons is habitually made, visible success becomes an end sought for its own utility as a basis of esteem" (Veblen 1899, 8). The value of visible success takes precedent over sufficient livelihood. Veblen further argued:

This visible difference between the old order and the new is closely dependent on the difference between the purposes that guide the older scheme of economic life and those of the new. Under the old order, industry, and even such trade as there was, was a quest of livelihood; under the new order industry is directed by the quest of profits. Formerly, therefore, times were good or bad according as the industrial processes yielded a sufficient or an insufficient output of the means of life. Latterly times are good or bad according as the process of business yields an adequate or inadequate rate of profits. The controlling end is different in the present, and the question of welfare turns on the degree of success with which this different ulterior end is achieved. Prosperity now means, primarily, business prosperity; whereas it used to mean industrial sufficiency.

(Veblen 1904, 60)

Veblen's observation of the changes to modern welfare is found to be imperative in the conservation of cultural shifts toward prosperity in the charro cowboy community.

Visible success in the charro cowboy community takes the form of trophies: physical and symbolic. This shift does not mean that all charro cowboys place visible success as their motivation to enact their tradition, as I will explain in Chapter 3. Nonetheless, it is worth explaining why an increasing number of charro cowboys find themselves concerned with opportunities to boost their visible success. Charro cowboy teams win prizes, plaques, and money. These physical prizes produce an incentive to continue winning and to continue competing. Symbolic trophies, like gaining recognition and prestige, also motivate teams and charro cowboy *jefes* to perform well during major *charreadas*. The power of business principles has transformed the charro cowboy community.

In particular, new problems have become more evident between the younger and older generations of charro cowboy. Charro cowboy *jefes* place growing pressure on their charro cowboy teams to win due to their own vested interest of gaining honor and status rather than just reproducing the charro cowboy tradition. Often this pressure has consequences on individual team members who find it hard to "keep up" with their boss' expectations. The peaceable intentions of the charro cowboy community to promote brotherhood, identity, and community are suppressed by the need to produce a profit. The predatory and barbaric characteristics of business principles place worth on the control of charro cowboy teams rather than individuals. Veblen states, "His control of the motions of other men is not strict, for they are not under coercion from him except through the coercion exercised by the exigencies of the situation in which their lives are cast…" (Veblen 1904, 2). The charro cowboy *jefe* and the Mexican Federation of Charros have contributed to the standardization of this tradition, thus causing teams to be similar to what Veblen called the machine process. This adaptation has strained the charro cowboy by reducing their freedom to actualize their idle curiosity.

Specifically, this distinction is visible in the younger generation of charro cowboys that have a "barbarian appreciation of worth or honor" while the older generation still possesses the more peaceable qualities of the tradition that preserves their values.

A charro cowboy is no longer considered successful by his ability to be versatile or independent, but by his ability to follow regulations enforced by the Mexican Federation of Charros. *Charreadas* in the charro cowboy community have transformed the instinct of workmanship by making it narrower and more directed to profit. Charro cowboy *jefes* and promoters benefit from the work of charro cowboy and their motives proceed from pecuniary gain. Veblen clearly explained that, "The modern industrial communities show an unprecedented uniformity and precise equivalence in legally adopted weights and measures" (Veblen 1904, 3). This uniformity is significant in the manifestation of this rural tradition, but it is not everything. Measure requires hierarchy and standardization. The charro cowboy tradition now more than ever has these modern industrial models embedded into its culture. While the desire to be a charro cowboy is a peaceable trait, the repercussion of business principles dictates the performance and enactment of the charro cowboy community.

## Charro cowboy *jefes* and the business motive

As Veblen argued, business principles mechanically regulate the livelihood of individuals and affect the welfare of society (Veblen 1904). The objective is for production to be efficient, so as to avoid idleness, waste, and hardship. These strategies of efficiency are adopted by some charro cowboy *jefes*. For example, Mario, a 62-year-old charro cowboy *jefe*, indicated proudly that he operates his team like a business. He is the charro cowboy *jefe* for the best performing and recognized team in the state of Jalisco. Mario's team is composed of winners who are often invited by the Mexican government to be present during Mexico's Independence Day and *National Day of the Charro*. His team consists of 20 charro cowboys of various socio-economic backgrounds that he has personally recruited over the years.

When asked about his recruitment style, Mario stated that he asked members of the Mexican Federation of Charros about possible recruits in smaller competition circuits. "There is always someone out there good enough to work for nothing." While his statement was delivered in a joking manner, there is an element of truth in his wording. Mario used coercion and chicanery by promising potential recruits fame and recognition in the charro cowboy community, especially for recruits with poor socio-economic backgrounds. Although a few members of Mario's team are highly recognized within the charro cowboy community, new team members tend to work on the ranch and only compete as alternates. Alternatives, as I will explain, end up doing the vast majority of the hard labor, often for little pay. Further, Mario funds his team with his own money and provides his team with horses and equipment.

The charro cowboy *jefe*'s main motive is pecuniary gain and status. Veblen stated, "The motive of business is pecuniary gain, the method is essentially purchase and sale. The aim and usual outcome is an accumulation of wealth. Men whose aim is not increase of possessions do not go into business, particularly not on an independent footing" (Veblen 1904, 7). All charro cowboy *jefes* share this particular ideology. Although Mario is a charro cowboy *jefe*, he rarely attends *charreadas* unless the *charreadas* are championship level events. Mario is not an active charro cowboy himself and he does not have any generational ties, but he has been drawn to the charro cowboy tradition because he was interested in charro cowboy music and livestock. His primary occupation is in advertising and the promotion of tequila vendors. His business interests overlap with the charro cowboy community since tequila is highly desired during *charreadas* and sold at every event. He is able to utilize the charro cowboy community for business purposes while maintaining profits in his own personal investments. Mario exemplifies the ideal barbarian with predatory habits that Veblen described. Veblen further argued, "In the sequence of cultural evolution the emergence of a leisure class coincides with the beginning of ownership" (Veblen 1899, 10). The charro cowboy *jefe* promotes the emergence of a more prominent leisure class within the charro cowboy community.

Mario is not an outlier in the charro cowboy community. In fact, he is part of a growing trend amongst the charro cowboy community managing teams with personal wealth in order to further his investments. In Veblen's chapter on modern business capital, he made the case that the management of modern business is disconnected from the constant visible control of the owner while ensuring the efficiency of workers. Veblen argued:

> This dissociation of the business control from workmanlike efficiency and from immediate contact with or ownership of the industrial plant gives the existing situation a superficial resemblance to the feudal system, in so far as touches the immateriality of the captain's connections with the everyday life and interests of the community of whose affairs he is master. It gives a certain plausibility to the attempted interpretation of the latter—day economic developments in feudalistic terms.
>
> (Veblen 1904, note 33)

Charro cowboy *jefes* own the necessary equipment, horses, practices spaces, etc. while their workers often own little or nothing. The labor of team members increases the value of the charro cowboy *jefe*'s investment without having team owners contribute their own time and labor. Veblen further argued, "The leisure of the master class is, at least ostensibly, an indulgence of a proclivity for the avoidance of labor and is presumed to enhance the master's own well-being and fullness of life; but the leisure of the servant class exempt from productive labor is in some sort a performance exacted from them, and is not normally or servant is not his own leisure" (Veblen 1899, 29). The charro cowboy *jefe* is able to demonstrate his visible success through owner-ship of a prestigious team. Since the charro cowboy *jefe* does not often par-ticipate in *charreadas*, the very fact that he owns the charro cowboy team provides him with the honor and status he very much desires. It is not his appreciation of the charro cowboy tradition that makes him honorable, but his ability to accumulate wealth.

Although the charro cowboy tradition advocates for frugal approaches to everyday life, many charro cowboys are inclined to purchase expensive horses to gain of prestige. Further, funding is needed to provide teams with suits, sombreros, boots, spurs, transportation, etc. These items are very expensive but necessary if a team wants to impress judges and adhere to the cultural expecta-tions of the charro cowboy tradition. Teams that do not have a charro cowboy *jefe* find themselves perceived as lack luster while their counterparts are praised for their flashy clothing. Throughout my fieldwork, I observed that 90% of charro cowboy judges paid close attention to teams with more expensive accoutrements such as horses, saddles, charro cowboy attire, etc. For example, judges would more often comment on the professionalism and elegance of these well funded teams than those operated by families, which is why charro cowboy *jefes* may be incentivized for their teams to have the same clothes and emblems on their equipment. This further reinforces the push for standardization despite many charro cowboys taking pride in their individuality in their presentation. These barbaric characteristics or habits of charro cowboy *jefes* suppress the peaceable characteristics of individual charro cowboys.

Charro cowboy *jefes* are often background figures or absentee owners that profit from the work of their charro cowboy workers because they do not compete or prepare for competitions. Veblen explained this aspect further when he stated, "This organization rests on the distinction between business management and ownership. The workmen do not and cannot own or direct the industrial equipment and processes, so long as ownership prevails and industry is to be managed on business principles" (Veblen 1904, 82). The distinction between charro cowboy *jefes* and charro cowboy team members is significant. Similar to how Veblen described that workmen could not own or direct the industrial equipment and processes, charro cowboys team members are also restricted by the ownership and direction of charro cowboy *jefes*. Many of them cannot afford to purchase expensive horses or saddles, there-fore rely heavily on the charro cowboy *jefe*'s investments. Charro cowboy *jefes* can be compared to corporate chief executive officers who profit from the actions of their workers, but do not actually *do* any of the hard labor.

Due to their wealthy backgrounds and upper class markers, charro cowboy *jefes* are exempt from hard labor. In the charro cowboy community, charro cowboy *jefes* represent an upper class that expresses leisure and conspicuous waste, reflecting their lack of utility to the greater Mexican society. Their association with the lower class is minimal. For example, the large amount of land that many charro cowboy *jefes* own is not worked by them, but rather by other groups of people that maintain the livestock.

In the case of Javier, a charro cowboy *jefe* from Mexico City, various workers that live on his land oversee his livestock. Javier's job and house is located about 30 minutes away and he only comes to the ranch at the weekend. Unlike Mario, Javier has a generational tie to the charro cowboy community and was a charro cowboy during his younger years, but suffered an injury that limited his ability to compete. He pays various members of his team to maintain and train the expensive horses that he provides for the competitions. This resonates with Veblen's discussion of ownership and wealth when he stated, "At this stage wealth consists chiefly of slaves, and the benefits accruing from the possession of riches and power take the form chiefly or personal service and the immediate products of personal service" (Veblen 1899, 19). The charro cowboy team cannot operate without the help the wealth of the charro cowboy *jefes* however, as Veblen indicated, this stage of wealth is made up of workers who are treated like indentured servants, in the sense that they are dependent on their labor to survive, since many charro cowboy workers cannot quit because they often owe their charro cowboy *jefes* a fair amount of money for equipment.

Charro cowboy *jefes* hire people from the nearby villages to work on their large ranches. On occasion, these workers are from a low socio-economic status and educational attainment, many holding only a middle school education. They view the charro cowboy community as a possible way of climbing the social ladder and gaining status. Charro cowboy *jefes* pay these individuals insignificant wages for strenuous labor and promise the opportunity to learn the charro cowboy tradition if they continue to work for their place on the team. In some cases, the worker is not paid but often loaned equipment such as a sombrero, boots, spurs, lassos, horses, saddles, etc. that he must work to repay with interest. Thus business practice can be best understood by Veblen when he stated, "The business man's object is to get the largest aggregate gain from his business" (Veblen 1904, 31). By loaning equipment, the charro cowboy *jefe* is able to secure the worker's loyalty and labor, requiring their workers to continuously depend on their labor to survive.

The charro cowboy *jefes* actively distinguish themselves from their teams by establishing their power through pecuniary means, thus reinforcing the social hierarchy. The investment is massive and also important, therefore, charro cowboy team members recognize that losing competitions could possibly lead to the end of their career with that particular team. This discovery can be better framed by Veblen's statement that, "The business man's place in the economy of nature is to 'make money,' not to produce goods. The production of goods is a mechanical process, incidental to the making of money; whereas the making of money is a pecuniary operation, carried on by bargain and sale, not by mechanical appliances and powers" (Veblen 1919, 92). Veblen argued that the primary goal of the businessman's investment is to turn a profit. The charro cowboy *jefe*'s motivation is also to make money rather than to "produce" the charro cowboy tradition, hence classifying their business operation similar to Veblen's understanding of business principles. Additionally, Veblen stated:

Investments are made for profit, and industrial plants and processes are capitalized on the basis of their profit—yielding capacity. In the accepted scheme of things among business men, profits are included as intrinsic to the conduct of business. So that, in place of the presumption in favor of a simple pecuniary stability of wealth, such as prevails in the rating of possessions outside of business traffic, there prevails within the range of business traffic the presumption that there must in the natural course of things be a stable and orderly increase of the property invested. Under no economic system earlier than the advent of the machine industry does profit on the investment seem to have accounted a normal or unquestionably legitimate source of gain.

(Veblen 1904, 27–28)

While the charro cowboy *jefe*'s operation is not a complete industry in the traditional sense, these teams conduct business presuming that the investment will be increased. The charro cowboy *jefes's* connection to the business world indicates that their main concern is about making money and gaining honor, and not enacting the charro cowboy tradition. Major competitions now have entry fees for competing teams, which are costly for teams with limited financial resources. Winners of these competitions not only gain prestige but also money and equipment. Therefore, winning is desirable for charro cowboy *jefes* because exposure and winning titles yields pecuniary gain. The charro cowboy *jefes* create an environment where winning is the most important goal because there is money to be made.

One particular example comes to mind to better frame this argument. In one case, one particular well-known charro cowboy *jefe*, Jesus, from central Mexico manages a prestigious charro cowboy team and owns a large rancho in central Mexico. Jesus is 78 years old and once served in a leadership role in the Mexican Federation of Charros. His charro cowboys were all recruits that his business partners had tracked over the years, a common practice amongst teams of high status. He was a ranch owner and made his money by selling livestock. Jesus had no previous familial ties to the charro cowboy community but his sons were now competing charro cowboys. Managing this team has generated revenue as his team is invited to *charreadas* across the country and many gained recognition for their charro cowboy skills. Since his team tended to win, they received many trophies and money throughout their careers with the team. During my time conducting fieldwork, the team continued to grow bigger and there were more alternatives available for charro cowboys that were unfit to compete.

Jesus, as a charro cowboy *jefe*, demanded a lot from his workers and team. Since charro cowboy team members are employees, there was an expectation that they would understand their position in the social hierarchy. Although not true servants, Veblen framed this expectation when he stated, "The first requisite of a good servant is the he should conspicuously know his place" (Veblen 1899, 29). Jesus's team recognized their place as employees and adhered to his every demand even if they did not necessarily agree with him. His team would never show their discontent, but it was clear from their comments in private that Jesus's expectations would often be too high.

The expectations of the charro cowboy *jefe* can create a toxic environment that can have serious consequences. One particular member of Jesus's team, Ivan, confessed that the demands of *El Jefe*, Jesus, often caused problems on the ranch. Ivan was a 32-year-old recovering alcoholic and stated that some of the charro cowboys were developed drug problems due to the demands of the charro cowboy *jefe*. He had seen instances when *El Jefe* Jesus's business partners offered amphetamines that they called "vitamins" to charro cowboys in order to ensure longer work hours and training sessions. Ivan recalls one particular incident when a team member was found training a horse until 5:00AM. The charro cowboy had taken these "vitamins" and had worked the horse to exhaustion. The horse could no longer perform in competitions due to this traumatic incident and had to be eventually put down. Jesus was notified about the incident and was more upset about the loss of the horse than his employee's health. Although this an extreme example, and there was no way for me to investigate the validity of Jesus' statements, this anecdote demonstrates the way in which charro cowboy *jefes* are driven by barbaric and predatory means rather than the peaceable elements of enacting and reproducing the charro cowboy tradition. However, throughout my fieldwork, I heard eight similar incidents from various charros of different high achieving teams.

## The charro cowboy team and social duty

Veblen stated, "A vested interest [as] a marketable right to get something for nothing. This does not mean that the vested interest cost nothing. These may even come at a high price. Particularly may their cost seem high if the cost to the community is taken into their account, as well as the expenditure incurred by their owners for their production and up-keep" (Veblen 1919, 100). Charro cowboy *jefes* have a vested interest because they "get something for nothing" through their large financial investments in the charro cowboy community. The majority do not participate in competitions, do not work on their own ranchos, and do not train their own horses.

Charro cowboys are employees that produce the charro cowboy tradition and feel pressure from charro cowboy *jefes* to strive for excellence. Often, the pressure to win prevents charro cowboys from pursuing their idle curiosity due to the fear of failure in competitions. The changes to the way the charro cowboy tradition is implemented has also played a role in the manner that charro cowboys compete. Specifically, the time regulation inhibits the charro cowboy team from focusing their attention on the animal or on their own safety. Since the emphasis is on winning, Charro cowboys center their actions on the expectations of the judges. I observed various occasions when an injury could have been avoided if the team had not been trying to beat the clock.

For example, *el paso de la muerte* or the pass of death is considered to be the fastest paced *suerte Charra* in the competition and one of the most dangerous. The Official and General Rules for Competitions 2012–2016 defines *el paso de la muerte* in the following way:

> This task consists of a charro cowboy riding bareback on a meek horse while attempting to jump to a brutish horse and facing forward; three charro cowboy will support the charro cowboy's run as jumper is subjected exclusively to grab the mane of the brutish horse. The jumper in this *suerte* starts from the moment he enters the *lienzo* and ends either when the rider dismounts gracefully, is shot down by the brute horse after he has jumped from one horse to another, falls on his initial meek horse in the attempt to complete the task, or when the three minutes to complete the task is up.
>
> (Federación Mexicana de Charreria, A.C. 2012–2016, 96)

Completing the task before the three-minute timer is essential to receive the maximum number of points and because this is the last event of the competition, there is a great incentive to score highly in order to ensure a victory. Extra points, ranging from 15 to 20, are awarded based on whether the jumper completes the pass in the first, second, or third run around the arena. Table 2.1 is a scoring template that charro cowboy judges use to assess the performance of the team. Judges evaluate charro cowboys based on how they conform to the charro cowboy tradition as well as the standardization implemented by the Mexican Federation of Charros. Infractions can range from causing the horse to bleed due to excessive use of spurs to failing to hold the *cuarta* whip correctly. Negative points can be awarded to competitors who fail to meet these expectations.

As the last *suerte* of the *charreadas*, this *suerte* is very important for a charro cowboy team trying to establish victory. This *suerte* can determine whether the charro cowboy team wins the prize money, new equipment, or is eliminated from competing in the national championships. Failing to complete *el paso de la muerte* results in the loss of ten points but there can also be more physical consequences. Failing to pass from one horse to another can result in falling under the horse's feet and getting trampled to death because the charro cowboy does not wear any protective gear other than his sombrero and vest. Death is the ultimate sacrifice, but serious injuries can occur that may debilitate the charro cowboy permanently or temporarily. Many jumpers have suffered from critical back injuries that have left them permanently injured. The jumping charro cowboy does not attempt this risky *suerte* by himself but is assisted by his team, who are responsible for helping him by forming a cluster of wranglers around him to direct the horse that way. Charro cowboy teams may help him by providing a forceful push if they feel that the jumper is taking too long to pass to from one horse to another.

Table 2.1 Scoring for El Paso de la Muerte

| Classification of the ride | Without the assistance of wrangler | Assistance of wrangler | Use of a riding quirt whip with the assistance of a wrangler | Use of a cuarta whip without the assistance of a wrangler | Dismounting while crossing both feet on one side or grabbing the horse ear to dismount | Landing with both feet on the ground without help from the team after the horse slows down | Failing to gracefully dismount |
|---|---|---|---|---|---|---|---|
| **Excellent** | 6 | 2 | 3 | 0 | 2 | 2 | 0 |
| **Good** | 4 | 2 | 2 | 0 | 1 | 1 | -1 |
| **Regular** | 2 | 0 | 1 | 0 | 0 | 0 | -2 |
| **Minimum** | 1 | 0 | 0 | 0 | 0 | 0 | -3 |

Note: This is an example of the scoring template translated from Spanish to English from the Mexican Federation of Charros' Official Rules for Competitions 2012–2016. This depicts the scoring for El Paso de la Muerte.

The following is a description of an incident that occurred during an *el paso del la muerte* attempt in Querétaro, Mexico:

> The charro cowboy prepares the horses for el paso de la muerte near the opening door of the lienzos. The jumper is securing his boots and wraps tape around his ankles and hands for support. He is wearing a protective vest in case he falls and the horse kicks him in the chest. He looks nervously into the crowd and then taps the top of his sombrero. His teammates position their horses around him. The team needs ten points to win the competition. They all look worried but ready to finish. The judges announce the team name loudly, "RANCHO AGUA SAGRADA!" The crowd claps and waits for the charro cowboys to start. The jumper prays for a few seconds, crosses himself, and points to the sky. He is ready. He signals his teammates and the wild mare is released into the arena. The horse sprints for thirty meters and the jumper struggles to find the right position to shift from one horse to another. He grabs the mane of the horse as he uses his cuarta whip to position his horse. He prepares himself. His teammates then push him forcefully and then the jumper hits his head hard onto a concrete post supporting a metal cover above. He is disoriented from the blow but not enough to stop. He successfully dismounts from his horse and the judges award him a total of eighteen points. He walks to his teammates and takes off his bent sombrero. He is bleeding from the blow and displays symptoms of a concussion. He wipes the blood from his forehead and gathers his things. They won and that's all that mattered.
>
> (Interview, May 2013)

His teammate attempted to stem the bleeding by pouring tequila on his forehead. This was successful but the charro cowboy most likely needed a few stitches. They wouldn't go the doctor until the very next morning. The charro cowboy in this vignette had a head injury, however the pressure to win was intense. Earlier that week, his charro cowboy *jefe* had emphasized that this win was essential for him to remain on the team. His teammates also felt this pressure and disregarded the safety of their fellow charro cowboys. When asked why they pushed the charro cowboy so forcefully, one team member explained that they felt that the jumper was taking too long to cross. Another explained that the jumper sometimes gets scared when the horses are running too fast therefore pushing him allows him to complete the task. It should be noted that the jumper is 18 years old and had only been competing at the professional level for a year. Accidents occur in the charro cowboy community all the time, however, this particular type of accident is a new development in the charro cowboy community.

The expectation to win is also demonstrated by the increased disregard for the welfare of animals. The charro cowboy tradition has always, according to many charro cowboys, considered the welfare of animals to be important. This was a firm belief among many charro cowboys who had strong generational ties to the community. There were several clauses in the Official and General Rules for Competitions 2012–2016 that deducted points from charro cowboys to prohibit the abuse of horses, cattle, and bulls. The charro cowboy tradition prides itself on the welfare of animals and this was the first thing that many charro cowboys told me during their interviews. This can be associated with the peaceable characteristics of the charro cowboy community that emphasize idle curiosity, examples of workmanship, and parental bent. Many charro cowboys, especially older and more experienced charro cowboys, often scold charro cowboy who injure horses or cattle during competitions and practice sessions.

The most common competition event where charro cowboys are more likely to be injured than their animals is during the *coleadero* or steer tailing. The *coleadero* is one the most popular *suertes* in the charro cowboy community because charro cowboys are able to display their masculine strength for the audience, who is able to witness their brute force in three attempts. This event takes a lot of upper body strength as well as balance and skill to execute correctly. It is not only a risk to the animals but can also lead to serious injury for the rider if something goes wrong. The practical use of this *suerte* is to prepare the bull to be branded. This technique was originally used in the colonial period. During competition portion of the *coleadero*, the charro cowboy has 30 seconds to grab the tail of the bull to proceed with the *suerte* after the charro cowboy judge determines that the bull is ready. The charro cowboy is judged and scored on how the bull falls, such as: full rotation to the right, full rotation to the left, middle right, middle left, on their stomach, heavy fall on its backside, or fall on its rear-end. The Official and General Rules for Competitions 2012–2016 demonstrates what the judges look for in terms of identifying the bull's fall and no fall is judged the same. Multiple points or bonus points are awarded on how fast the bull was dropped and if the fall yielded multiple rotations. The charro cowboy is not supposed to hurt the bull or their horse in this *suerte* and can have points deducted for slamming the horse too hard against the wall before take off or reprimanding the horse in a physical manner. Mistakes can be detrimental to the charro cowboy, the horse, and the bull.

In a particular incident, a charro cowboy of about 35 years old (José) was performing the *colas en el lienzo* or the steer tailing of a bull. José is well known for his ability to carry out the *colas en el lienzo* and often is the favorite to win. During one competition, José prepared himself at the entrance of the gate. The charro cowboy is required to greet the judges with a nod before he starts the *suerte* and wait for the signal from them confirming that he can proceed. José received the signal from the judges and then forcefully pressed his spurs against his horse's body, leaving a small indent of blood on the horse's side. He had 30 seconds to grab the bull's tail but struggled to firmly hold it in his hand. In a panic, he grabbed the tail of the bull and pulled it too far back behind him. He was aiming for the maximum amount of points, but by pushing the bull too close to his horse's hind legs, he injured his own horse badly. A loud haunting crack could be heard throughout the *lienzo*. Everyone was silent because they knew that the horse could never recover from such a hard blow to the leg. The horse stopped and lifted his left foot in pain. The *lienzo* was quiet and everyone in the audience witnessed the last few hours of the horse's life. A team of veterinarians, usually present during formal competitions, ran into the *lienzo* as they tried to help the horse to an isolated stall near the back of the *lienzo*. José had broken his horse's leg badly, but had gotten the bull to roll twice for the maximum amount of points. He was ashamed that he had hurt the horse's foot badly, and therefore did not make eye contact with the judges or anyone else. In the pursuit of glory, he had broken the foot of his charro cowboy *jefe's* best horse. Although he would have to wait to be reprimanded from his charro cowboy *jefe*, he was subjected to the older and more experienced charro cowboys shouting, "Mr. Break" and "You're a garbage of Charro" that continued until the end of the night.

This particular event is consistent with the consequences of the dominance of business principles in terms of profit, glory, and investment. Veblen further argues, "Before business principles came to dominate everyday life the common welfare, when it was not a question of peace and war, turned on the case and certainty with which enough of the means of life could be supplied" (Veblen 1904, 59). Due to the increased influence of business principles in the operation of the charro cowboy tradition, the welfare of animals and charro cowboys has been ignored because of organizations such as the Mexican Federation of Charros' push for standardization and the emphasis on prestige and honor. In addition, charro cowboy *jefes* have pushed for their vested interests causing a tension between the peaceable traits of the charro cowboy community and the competing barbaric traits: a clear indication that the peaceable traits are not eliminated but suppressed. Although the charro cowboy community pushes for the welfare of charro cowboys and their animals to be a significant and constant requirement, these concerns are deemed less important than the pressure to win and make a profit. Charro cowboys recognize this urgency and operate according to what their absentee owners request of their teams. The infringing principles of business are also causing derangement within the charro cowboy community. Veblen describes derangement as the disturbance of the equilibrium between peaceable and barbaric habits at any particular point. The charro cowboy community has been divided between those that support the business principles of the charro cowboy *jefes* and charro cowboy teammates that still have the instinct of workmanship, parental bent, and idle curiosity with regard to the charro cowboy tradition. Further division is evident within charro cowboy teams due to generational differences.

### Generational differences in the charro cowboy community

"CHARROS DE SAN ANTONIO!" yells a short man of about forty into the microphone as a group four charro cowboy make their way into the center of the thermometer shaped arena. The charro cowboy prepares to compete, as it is their team's turn to attempt the Manganas a Caballo or the foreleg horse catch from horseback. The leader signals the other charro cowboy with a forceful wave and they all split in their positions as a wild mare is released into the area. A large cloud of dirt slowly rises into the air as three charro cowboy sprint on their horses across the arena trying to manipulate the fast pace of the wild mare. OOH! ORALE! VAMOS! They scream loudly as the spring in a circle. A single charro cowboy remains steady on his horse as the other sprint around the circle. The single charro cowboy looks at the wild mare and targets his lariat to the feet of the horse. He swings the lariat side to side and then he makes a full circle above his head bringing the circular motion closer to the body of the horse. His swings are beautiful and almost magical to watch as he jumps from side to side at the spinning circle of his lariat. His muscles work hard to prepare for this catch. He is focused. He is ready. The wild mare sprints once past him. As the wild mare approaches for a final turn, the charro cowboy launches his trap catching the front two feet of the wild mare. He pulls the lariat forcefully closer to the hook of his saddle and rapidly ties the lariat around it. The twine on the horn of the saddle fiercely breaks from the intensity of the pull. The movement is quick, dramatic, yet successful. The wild mare falls and the crowd roars with applause. The successful charro cowboy turns his head and lifts his sombrero to the three judges on the left side of the arena.

(Observation, July 2013)

This vignette depicts a moment of glory for a young charro cowboy trying to impress the judges, his charro cowboy *jefes*, and the audience. Many young charro cowboys are motivated by promises of prestige and leisure from the higher class charro cowboys. Although issues of class stratification within the charro cowboy community have always been present, class divisions are read differently among generational lines. The peaceable characteristics of the charro cowboy community are less visible in the younger generation of charro cowboys than in the older generation. The difference seems to be the result of where and how charro cowboys are socialized. The older generation of charro cowboys was more likely to have grown up in rural communities while the younger generation was more likely to have been socialized in urban areas of Mexico. Young charro cowboys are submerging themselves in the charro cowboy community at a time when there is a clear strain regarding what makes a charro cowboy authentic. Further, many young charro cowboy were socialized from a young age to modern amenities such as electricity, running water, and televisions and are less likely to have a personal narrative to the rural traditions of a small charro cowboy town. The smaller rural towns in Mexico tend to have less access to these amenities. Although Mexico can be associated with developing characteristics, its economic adjustment through-out the last 50 years has led to rapid industrialization and urbanization throughout the country (Lustig 1998; Gutmann 1996). Due to these changes, charro cowboy competitions now consist of more modern elements than ever before such as large display screens, digital streaming, and digital clocks.

Socialization is essential to the preservation of the charro cowboy community. This socialization is not uniform and depends on the cultural and social character of the present society. Social character types, as theorized by David Riesman (1961), have an effect on employment, leisure, politics, and the child-rearing activities of society. Since Mexico has undergone social, institutional, and economic changes, it is only right to assume that Mexico has also undergone social character changes. It is important to analyse these generational differences and shifts through Riesman's work because they provide an additional framing to the influence of business principles. Riesman was a scholar of Veblen and his theoretical paradigm provides the necessary cultural tool to understand why there is a generational shift in the charro cowboy community that values more barbaric and predatory cultural habits.

Although social character types may dominate a milieu, social types are not permanent and can be applied to generational differences. Riesman (1961) argued that there are three social character types: *Tradition-directed, inner-directed,* and *other-directed.* Riesman stated in regards to inner-direction, "the source of direction for the individual is 'inner' in the sense that it is implanted early in life by the elders and directed toward generalized by nonetheless inescapably destined goals" (Riesman 1961, 21). For example, most of the older generation of charro cowboys do not focus on mastering the charro cowboy tradition for the purpose of glory or recognition but out of respect of the tradition. While there are various older and notable charro cowboys that have gained recognition throughout the years, their reputation was centered on commitment to the charro cowboy tradition and making sure their traditions lived on. The older generation of charro cowboy is inner-directed because of their rural upbringing. Their rural parents predominantly set their metaphorical gyroscope, which shapes their behaviour as adults (Riesman 1961, 45). Riesman stated:

> The inner-directed cynic is or can be an opportunist, ruthless in pursuing his goals. Or he may be a disgruntled idealist, still in practice committed to rectitude. In pursuit of his aims, good bad, he may be quite ready to exploit others, just as the inner-directed moralizer may be quite ready to force others to be moral, too.
>
> (Riesman 1961, 195)

While the older generation of charro cowboys has every capacity to exploit others in the same way as the younger generation of charro cowboys, their goal is mostly centered on the reproduction and continuity of their tradition.

Juan is a 71-year-old charro cowboy from Mexico City. He has spent his entire life working on his small ranch located 20 minutes outside Mexico City. His ranch is between two other properties that focus on agriculture rather than cattle. His ranch is not very big but he manages the upkeep of his land with the help of his adult son. He owns a few horses but nothing close to a charro cowboy *jefe*. He owns a few bulls that he sells to the local markets if his finances are precarious. Juan's primary source of income is his ability to train horses for *charreadas*. His charro cowboy skills are impressive and he very much enjoys working with horses. Occasionally, Juan will compete in individual charro cowboy competitions that do not require a team however his participation has decreased due to multiple back injuries that inhibit his skills. He has a true sense of what Veblen would characterize as the instinct of workmanship because he has never missed a day of work. He was born in a small village of about 100 people in the state of Jalisco. His father was charro cowboy but did not compete in formal competitions. Juan learned the charro cowboy tradition by working with his father and his six other brothers on the ranch. Although he comes from a low socio-economic background, he achieved his dream of owning his ranch and becoming a competing charro cowboy like his father. Introduction to the competitive charro cowboy sphere occurred in the 1970s when his brother began competing professionally and invited Juan to join him. Juan represents the older generation of charro cowboys that are more interested in the tradition than in winning.

The generational ties to the charro cowboy tradition are very revealing. The emphasis on tradition by the older generation also allows many charro cowboys to believe that the charro cowboy tradition should be reserved for those who come from charro cowboy familial ties. When asked if any person could be a charro cowboy, Samuel, a 51-year-old charro cowboy stated:

> My grandfather was a great horseback rider. My father is a great horseback rider. My father, I think was better. [My father] is seventy-eight years old and he is known as Charro Don Major. He started [practicing charro cowboy tradition] at eighteen as a professional and now is a legacy. Everyone knows how much he had done for [the charro cowboy tradition]. My father is great because it is in his blood. It's in my blood. My father started from nothing. His success, his success is based on the love for the animals. Charros. Tequila. (laughs). I tell my sons, nephews, and grandchildren that if they want to be men…get on that horse. No one can be [a charro cowboy] just like that. Being a charro is from the soul.
>
> (Interview, August 2014)

Samuel's statement is telling of an inner-directed perspective. His desire to be a charro cowboy was a family necessity but his decision to compete was due to his own determination to express his traditional connection further. The charro cowboy tradition, Samuel's description, is associated with what Veblen regards as the instinct of workmanship. His family has dedicated their entire lives to the charro cowboy tradition and believe that true charro cowboy legitimacy comes from being born into the community.

Bloodlines are very important to older generations of charro cowboys because it validates the tradition's origins of rural communities. As Riesman argued, the inner-directed character is "very considerably bound by traditions: they limit his ends and inhibit his choice of means" (Riesman 1961, 16). The charro cowboy is bound by a tradition that conveys the instinct of workmanship, idle curiosity, and parental bent in relation to horsemanship skills. Additionally, Riesman states, "Even if the individual's choice of tradition is largely determined for him by his family, as it is in most cases, he cannot help become aware of the existence of competing tradition—hence of tradition as such" (Riesman 1961, 16). The competing tradition is the charro cowboy leisure class that includes the charro cowboy *jefes*, tequila investors, and famous charro cowboy. Veblen stated, "Under common-sense barbarian appreciation of work or honor, the taking of life—the killing formidable competitors, whether brute or human—is honorable in the highest degree" (Veblen 1899, 9). The emerging leisure class in the charro cowboy community holds a barbarian appreciation of prestige or honor while those charro cowboys who are considered to be lower class have more peaceable attributes due to their inability to sufficiently exploit others.

In the example of Samuel, he was exposed to competing Mexican traditions when he moved to Mexico City in his early 30s. He continued his involvement in the charro cowboy community even though the city was not convenient for practicing the tradition. Although he makes up the older generation of charro cowboys, his children and grandchildren have been exposed to the newer developments of the charro cowboy community. His children associate themselves more with the business principles of the Charro tradition rather than the original peaceable attributes of the instinct of workmanship, parental bent, and idle curiosity. Although Samuel's goal during *charreadas* is to enjoy the company of other charro cowboys, his children and grandchildren strive to win competitions and make money as the motivating factor to continue in their family tradition. Samuel spent most of his time on the ranch caring for his animals while his sons hire local teenagers to watch over their horses and cattle while they enjoy their free time. While Samuel is not interested in becoming part of the charro cowboy leisure class, his sons center their daily activity around achieving leisure class status. Veblen stated, "The leisure class lives by the industrial community rather than in it. Its relations to industry are of a pecuniary rather than industrial kind" (Veblen 1899, 113). As Veblen theorized, those who want to achieve leisure class status and honor are more interested in the pecuniary gain rather than serviceability. Samuel's sons embody barbaric and predatory habits of exploitation that is indicative of an inner-directed social character in the younger generation of charro cowboys.

As mentioned previously, the older charro cowboy generation does compete in national charro cowboy competitions throughout Mexico. There are competitions reserved exclusively for older charro cowboys throughout the year that are promoted by the Mexican Federation of Charros. During these competitions, the older charro cowboys compete in the same series of *suertes* or tasks, however, they spend their free time drinking tequila, smoking cigars or cigarettes, and catching up with old friends. The early *charreadas* were about brotherhood and celebrations between adjacent villages, and the remnants of these characteristics are still present today. Many older charro cowboys do not feel the stress of winning because winning is not the goal of their participation, but rather the special camaraderie. During charro cowboy competitions, it is not rare to see a group of older charro cowboys laughing and drinking on their horses while they wait their turn in the competition line-up. Many older and experienced charro cowboys focus on their own personal goals during *charreadas* rather than a goal set by a charro cowboy *jefe*. Their skills are often refined therefore they care more about exceeding their own expectations while staying true to the charro cowboy tradition. This does not mean that older charro cowboys are not found in well funded teams, instead they are less likely to care about the expectations of the charro cowboy boss because they hold more confidence in their skills.

In addition, the older charro cowboy generation often host their own informal competitions at their ranchos that are not sponsored by the Mexican Federation of Charros. These informal gatherings mimic the traditional *charreadas* of the past because there is no enforcement of standardization through time limits, measurements, or charro cowboy judges. Charro cowboys that are invited to these informal events are friends and family of the hosting charro cowboy. Although these are informal competitions that are often characterized as practice sessions, the participating charro cowboys will bring food and drinks for everyone present. There will be plenty of tequila and cigarettes for all. In one particular situation, a charro cowboy brought goat meat from his ranch to roast over a fire to make tacos. While the charro cowboy men enjoyed themselves out on the *lienzo*, the charro cowboy wives worked hard to make tacos for the entire group and watched over smaller children. It should also be noted that these informal competitions tend to be hosted by older generation of charro cowboy because they are more likely to have the space and resources to host these gatherings. However, the younger generation of charro cowboy that have the financial means to host a similar event will not do so if the event will not yield financial beneficial. The older generation of charro cowboys act upon their tradition that promotes brotherhood and community.

When asked what is different about modern *charreadas*, several older charro cowboys argued that technology has now been included within the community, which both helps and inhibits the charro cowboy community. Specifically, large television screens that project the statistics of the competition as well as replay shots of particular *suertes* are present in the more prestigious national competitions. This coincides with standardization and the influence of business principles that Veblen argued relating to technology as well as the dominance of what Riesman called "screen culture".

Although older and experienced charro cowboys were positive about the benefits of technology, the majority of the older of charro cowboys claimed that organizers were trying to make the tradition similar to soccer. Pedro, a 67-year-old charro cowboy, complained that the charro cowboy tradition is not about replays or statistics. "Replay is bullshit. I do not want to see how many times this charro messed up. I do not want to see it at all." Statistics projected on a giant screen cause anxiety for competing charro cowboys that want to satisfy the expectations of their charro cowboy *jefes*. Further, replaying mistakes and accidents distracts charro cowboys and the audience from original purpose of the tradition, to enjoy their culture. While the older generation of charro cowboys seem relaxed and calm from a distance, the younger generation of charro cowboys look anxious and stressed about their impending performance. These giant screens take a lot of time to install and are very costly for the Mexican Federation of Charros. In my observations, the screens served as more a distraction because the flashy graphics took away attention from competitors and even the announcements of the charro cowboy judges.

The younger generation of charro cowboys consists of a mixture of legacy charro cowboys and first generation charro cowboys. As mentioned, many younger charro cowboy competitors feel the pressure of charro cowboy *jefes* and feel that the older generation do not care enough about winning national titles. Riesman argued, "The inner-directed person becomes capable of maintaining a delicate balance between the demands upon him on his goal in life and the buffetings of his external environment" (Riesman 1961, 16). The older generation of charro cowboys understood how to balance their goals and the external environment, however this is not true for many young charro cowboys. Rather, the younger generation of charro cowboys can be considered to be more other-directed in social character. Unlike inner-directed social character types that gain a feeling of control over their own lives, Riesman explained that other-directed social character types are directed by the environment of people. Riesman stated, "What is common to all the other-directed people is that their contemporaries are the source of direction for the individual—either those known to him or those who whom he is indirectly acquainted, through friends and through the mass media" (Riesman 1961, 21). Although some older charro cowboys can have other-directed inclinations, it is evident that the younger generation of charro cowboys exhibit more other-directed qualities. Neither their parents nor the charro cowboy tradition influence their goals. The principle desire is to be like other winning charro cowboys that they admire and associate themselves within the charro cowboy leisure class.

The allure of the charro cowboy leisure class is much more attractive to the other-directed charro cowboy because of the honor and perceived respect that charro cowboy *jefes* are given by the Mexican Federation of Charros. The charro cowboy *jefe* lifestyle is luxurious and many younger charro cowboys find themselves trying to emulate them because of the belief that they are the epitome of success. As previously argued, charro cowboy *jefes* belong to a charro cowboy leisure class due to their conspicuous consumption and lack of generational legitimacy to the tradition. The younger generation of charro cowboys notice that charro cowboy *jefes* have large ranches and expensive equipment that is not found among poorer members. Further, charro cowboy teams are able to enjoy the wealth of the Charro *jefes* through vicarious leisure due their connection to the charro cowboy *jefe*'s control. Veblen better frames this cultural framing in his statement:

> In so far as this is true the labor spent in these services is to be classed as leisure; and when performed by others than the economically free and self-directing head of the establishment, they are to be classed as vicarious leisure. The vicarious leisure preformed by housewives and menials, under the head of the household cares, may frequently develop into drudgery, especially where the competition for reputability is close and strenuous.
>
> (Veblen 1889, 28)

Teams, particularly compromised of younger charro cowboys, receive the benefits of the charro cowboy *jefe*'s wealth even though they preform the drudgery or hard labor. They have access to expensive and well-trained horses, authentic silver spurs, space to practice, etc. The younger generation of charro cowboys are often preoccupied with having the "right type of clothing" and the "right type of horse" besides just replicating the very culture that they inhabit.

These are not the interests of the older generation of charro cowboys. Wealthy young charro cowboys spend large quantities of money on clothing worn by famous charro cowboys in the competition circle to elevate themselves in their charro cowboy peers' judgmental eyes. Those younger charro cowboys will spend their limited budgets on acquiring luxury clothing and equipment in order to blend in with their charro cowboy peers. The older generation of charro cowboys with generational ties usually wear attire that was handmade by their family members or have been passed down. In addition, older charro cowboys are often seen wearing the same charro cowboy attire for years since they do not place much emphasis on luxury charro cowboy clothing, as long as their self-presentation satisfies the requirements presented in the Official and General Rules for Competitions 2012–2016.. When asked about what they thought about charro cowboys who focus on clothing, they laughed. One older charro cowboy expressed, "It's almost like they are women. They have to have the newest fashion." The attire of the older generation of charro cowboys typically possess a deep historical significance because these Charro clothes often resemble the suits worn by the first charro cowboys in the 1920s. Older charro cowboys do not use the charro cowboy attire to distinguish themselves from the charro cowboy community but rather to demonstrate their membership.

Sombreros are also a very important feature to the charro cowboy self-presentation. The older generation of charro cowboys tended to have sombreros that were dirty from the ranch because they wore them all the time. Sombreros cover the face from the sun as well as protect the head in the event of a fall. They are not used for fashion purposes. Yet, young and wealthy charro cowboys have custom-made sombreros that are made from the best materials for the sole purpose of competing. These sombreros can cost hundreds and even thousands of dollars to make, often made from real rabbit fur and threaded with gold. Even the simplest sombreros can cost a whole month's salary. Their self-presentation represents conscious consumption since their charro cowboy attire displays their social class status or perceived social status. Generational differences are apparent in the condition of the charro cowboy suit and even the type of sombrero. For example, younger generations of charro cowboys tend to wear their sombreros only for *charreadas*. There was a growing trend of having team emblems embroidered on to the sombreros furthering displaying their status and in some cases, connection to charro cowboy *jefes*. Although the younger generation of charro cowboys emulate the self-presentation of other charro cowboys, their other-directed social character also drives younger charro cowboys to duplicate the performance of others. Regional differences also allow some younger charro cowboys to opt for more prestigious sombreros representative of their home states. This is the case for some charro cowboys from Jalisco who often wear taller and straw like sombreros whose origin dates back to the colonial period.

Further, since *charreadas* for the younger generation of charro cowboys place emphasis on victories, many young charro cowboys will jeopardize their own skills in order to avoid failure as well as possible unemployment. This can be framed as a consequence of the standardization of the charro cowboy business principles. For example, Gustavo is a 27-year-old charro cowboy with generational ties. Although his father grew up in a small ranch outside of Pachuca, Gustavo grew up in the city. He was required to work on the ranch with his father at an early age until he earned his college degree in his early adulthood. Gustavo's charro cowboy *jefe* is a wealthy businessman that he met through his father's friend. His charro cowboy team is well respected among the Mexican Federation of Charros and performs well during competition season. Gustavo is a *charro completo* or a complete charro cowboy. A *charro completo* has the expertise to perform all nine *suertes* or events, which is a skill that not all charro cowboys possess. Although the label of *charro completo* was the standard in colonial Mexico, charro cowboys are less likely to label themselves as a *charro completo* and specialize in one or two specific *suertes*. Although the Mexican Federation of Charros hosts several competitions throughout Mexico specifically for *charro completos*, the same cluster of *charro completos* tend to participate at each event. Modern charro cowboys, in particular the younger generation, acknowledge the difficulty of mastering all nine *suertes*.

Although Gustavo has the skills to compete in every *charreadas* as a *charro completo*, he actively chooses not to compete as such because of his desire to be a team player. Gustavo competes in the *suerte* called the *jineteo de yegua* or bareback mare riding. In this particular *suerte*, the charro cowboy will have up to six minutes to accomplish the task of removing two ties from the bucking mare. The goal of the *jineteo de yegua* is to remain mounted on the back of the mare until it stops bucking and then gracefully dismount without falling. Judges award points based on time completed, quality of the rider, and the dismount. Gustavo can focus his attention on performing well on this specific *suerte* rather than performing well on every *suerte* in the *charreada*. He avoids potential replacement if he is responsible for performing badly in every *suerte* and costing his team the winning title. The older generation of charro cowboys argue that the fear of failure causes younger charro cowboys to sabotage their talents. Veblen argues that the use of sabotage is a common practice within vested interest and business principles. He states, "Workmen have resorted to such measures to secure improved conditions of work, or increased wages, or shorter hours, or to maintain their habitual standards, to all of which they have claimed to have some sort of vested right. Any strike is of the nature of sabotage, of course" (Veblen 1919). Similar to Veblen's analysis, young charro cowboys recognize that the charro cowboy *jefes* would expect them to realize their full potential each time they competed therefore they sabotage their own skills in order to secure their work and wages. *Charro completos*, like Gustavo, would rather specialize in a particular *suerte* and jeopardize their skills than make themselves vulnerable to failure or unemployment.

Veblen argued that the business enterprise reduced the craftsmanlike skill to mechanical standardization. This is because products or skills, in this case, need to be yield the most cost effective outcome for the businessman or charro cowboy *jefe*. There is little room for error in charro competitions and *charro completos* take a gamble when they choose to compete in every event because they are expected to be equally skilled and talented in every one. Since the charro cowboy *jefe* is more focused on efficiency and success, charro cowboys recognize that noncompliance might lead to losing. Veblen discussed this point when he stated:

> A disturbance at any point, whereby any given branch of industry fails to do its hare in the work of the system at large, immediately affects the neighbouring or related branches which come before or after it in the sequence, and is transmitted through their derangement to the remoter portions of the system. The disturbance is rarely confined to the single plant or the single line of production first affected, but spreads in some measure to the rest. A disturbance at any given point brings more or less derangement to the industrial process at large.
>
> (Veblen 1904, 6)

The prevention of this is essential for those individuals who profit from the charro cowboy tradition. While Veblen was referring to standardization as it relates to industry in the United States, his argument is applicable here. The fear of losing yields a particular type of anxiety within the younger generation of charro cowboys.

The younger generation of charro cowboys are also anxious about performing well. Unlike the older generation of charro cowboys that view competitions as celebrations, younger charro cowboys view competitions as work. The tradition is transformed into tasks that need to be mastered for the purpose of winning a competition rather than keeping culture alive. The barbaric elements due to the influence of business principles negatively influence the new generation of charro cowboys by suppressing their idle curiosity, parental bent, and instinct of workmanship. Their idle curiosity is suppressed because of their growing fear of failing others. For example, Humberto, an 18-year-old charro cowboy, described his relationship with the charro cowboy community as stressful. He stated, "I hate disappointing the team. I want to experiment with my movement...my horse and I have been practicing...practicing other strategies. I can't do it because that's not what [the charro cowboys *jefe*] wants." Humberto was experiencing the suppression of his idle curiosity. During his practice sessions, he seemed more relaxed and able to perform the *suertes* the way he wanted to because he was not directed by any authority or others. There was no judge. There was no charro cowboy *jefe*. He was free to ride his horse and experiment with his movements. The anxiety returned with the presence of his team and his anxiety was noticeable in his demeanor. He would conform to the direction of others and was very focused on meeting their expectations.

The older generation of charro cowboys notice that the younger generation operated with fear to fit the expectations of charro cowboy *jefes* and with each other. When asked about their thoughts of the younger generation, most older and experienced charro cowboys proclaimed, "*estos chamacos no saben* (these kids don't know)" in relation to the tradition. The older generation of charro cowboys noticed the growing concern of the younger generation to appease other charro cowboys rather than upholding the traditions of their family. Riesman stated, "...it matters very much who these 'others' are: whether they are the individual's immediate circle or a 'higher' circle or the anonymous voices of the mass media; whether the individual fears the hostility of chance acquaintances or only of those who 'count'" (Riesman 1961, 22). The other-directed nature of the younger generation of charro cowboys triggered their anxiety by causing them to conform to their peers rather than keeping the tradition alive. The younger generation of charro cowboys tends to place value on the opinion of their peers, slowly destroying the original purpose of the charro cowboy tradition. The growing influence of mass media such as Instagram, Facebook, WhatsApp, etc. among the younger generation will be addressed further in the upcoming chapters. Although the younger generation demonstrate the most cultural adaptation due to their adoption of charro cowboy business principles and other-directed social character, this does not mean that the older generation of charro cowboys is completely immune to these changes. However, the older generation is more resistant to change due to their charro cowboy generational ties and rural upbringing.

Veblen's theoretical arguments regarding standardization, pecuniary gain, barbaric and predatory culture, the instinct of workmanship, idle curiosity, and parental bent allows for the explanation of some of the new problems within the charro cowboy community. In particular, Veblen's argument regarding the power of business principles provides clarity to why charro cowboy *jefes* have growing importance and influence over the younger generation of competing charro cowboys. *Charro cowboy jefes* place new pressures on teams for their own vested interests rather than the peaceable intensions of the community. Further, charro cowboy *jefes* now comprise a growing charro cowboy leisure class that influences how charro cowboys view success. The charro cowboy team often compromised their talents and skills in order to conform to the needs of the team and causing them to sabotage their own skills for the desire to win. The older generation notice the differences in the younger generation's behaviour, which they consider to be below par of the charro cowboy tradition. In the next chapter, I will address construction of the charro cowboy identity and the role of women in the charro cowboy community.

## Note

1 There are a total of nine *suertes Charras* in a single *charreadas*: 1. *Cala de Caballo* (Reining) 2. *Piales en Lienzo* (Heeling) 3. *Colas en el Lienzo* (Steer Tailing) 4. *Jineteo de Toro* (Bull Riding) 5. *Terna en el Reudo* (Team Roping) 6. *Jineteo de Yegua* (Bareback on a wild mare) 7. *Manganas de Caballo* (Forefooting) 8. *Manganas a Caballo* (Fore booting on Horseback) 9. *El Paso de la Muerte* (The pass of death).

## References

Federación de Charros, A.C. *Reglamentos Generales para Competencias.* Mexico City:, 2012–2016.

Gutmann, Matthew C., *The Meanings of Macho: Being a Man in Mexico City.* Berkley, California: University of California Press. 2007[1996] .

Lustig, Nora, *Mexico the Remaking of an Economy.* 2nd ed. Washington, D.C.: Brookings Institution Press. 1998.

O'Hara, Phillip A. "Veblen's Analysis of Business, Industry and the Limits of Capital: An Interpretation and Sympathetic Critique." *History of Economics Review* vol. 20 (1993): 95–119.

Ramírez Barreto, Ana Cristina. "Defendiendo animales, redefiniendo tradiciones. Cómo charros y charras en California enfrentan las acciones legales contra eventos de la charreada." In *De humanos y otros animals,* 195–199. México: Editorial Dríada. 2009.

Riesman, David, *The Lonely Crowd: A Study of the Changing American Character.* New Haven, Connecticut: Yale University Press. 1961.

Veblen, Thorstein. *The Instinct of Workmanship, and the State of the Industrial Arts.* New York: A.M. Kelley, Bookseller. 1964[1919].

Veblen, Thorstein. *The Theory of Business Enterprise.* New York: A.M. Kelley, Bookseller. 1965[1904].

Veblen, Thorstein. *The Theory of the Leisure Class: An Economic Study of Institutions.* New York: Reprint by The New American Library, 1953[1899].

Veblen, Thorstein *The Vested Interest and the Common Man.* New York: Reprint by Augustus M Kelley Pubs. 1963[1920].

# 3 The modern charro cowboy ambition and fantasy

> We arrive at the *lienzo* around 11:36AM. The *charreada* does not begin until 1:00PM but there is so much to do. There are about six large trailers full of horses ready for competitions. Some are plain white, while others are marked with emblems of some of the most recognized teams in Mexico. Ranch hands, mostly young men, quickly beginning their work by making sure the animals are taken care of. They make sure the horses are walked, fed, and prepared for a long day of *charreando*. Gerardo, a 35-year-old charro cowboy, takes his horse from his worker, Miguel, and begins to saddle it up. His son, Gerardo Jr. of about six years old, walks up to him and attentively watches his father work. He waits patiently as his father signals him so he can warm up the horse. Although Gerardo Jr. is only six years old, he has been riding horses practically his whole life. His mother, Silvia, smiles as she brushes her hair next to the truck and applies some makeup on her face. Con cuidado! "With caution!" she yells. Gerardo places his son on the horse and directs him to the *lienzo*. Gerardo Jr. flashes his father a huge smile as his feet dangle a foot from the stirrups. The young boy demonstrates confidence when managing the towering horse and tightly holds the reigns in his tiny hands as he steers the horse. He shows minimal anxiety but truly enjoys his moment. He gallops towards the rest of the charro cowboy sons before flashing another smile in the direction of father…It will not be very long until Gerardo Jr. will be competing in his very own *charreada*.
>
> (Interview, May 2014)

Socialization in the charro cowboy tradition starts early for many young aspiring charro cowboys. In the case of Gerardo, his son has been exposed to horses since he was an infant. Gerardo Jr.'s very first appearance at a *charreada* was at only four months old and since then, he has rarely missed the opportunity to watch his father compete with his charro cowboy team. Although the customs and traditions of the charro cowboy community are not the mainstream cultural sentiments of the greater Mexican population, those who participate in the charro cowboy community are dedicated to its discipline, culture, and traditions. As previously stated, the community formed as a rebellious counterculture against Spanish colonialism and as a way to take ownership of their marginal identity. Initially the charro cowboy community welcomed those individuals who wished to up keep their tradition, but as the generational ties to the charro cowboy community gained more importance than the inclination to participate, problems regarding legitimacy emerged. These differences emerged as a consequence of the diminishing importance of rural life and the rise of individuals using the charro cowboy tradition to elevate their status in society. These differences class and generational tie differences within the charro cowboy tradition stem from the divisions created by the upper and ruling class prior to the Mexican Revolution (Sands 1993). The older generation explained the significance of bloodlines as a necessary perquisite for "belonging" in the charro cowboy community. "Blood" to these charro cowboys forge the link between one charro cowboy generation and another. This becomes a powerful tool to discriminate newcomers or individuals deemed unworthy of the charro cowboy label.

The charro cowboy tradition is typically passed down from generation to generation through male children. In previous generations, charro cowboy teams comprised primarily families with the charro cowboy pedigree. Charro cowboy children learn and practice the charro cowboy *suertes,* a series of rodeo style events, and some even compete in *charreadas* sponsored by the Mexican Federation of Charros. These aspiring underage charro cowboys go through a specific socialization process into the community that is not experienced by potential charro cowboy with no generational ties. Access into the community for these non-generational charro cowboys is harder and their socialization process is unlike those with generational ties. "Belonging" in the charro cowboy community creates obstacles for those who have a genuine interest in the charro cowboy tradition yet have no current or past connection. Further, continuous marginalization is more prominent among indigenous and lower class charro cowboy rookies. In particular, issues of classism and colorism have become real problems for many competing charro cowboys with no generational ties to the community. This causes continuous marginalization of charro cowboys that are labeled as "illegitimate" by others. They are often denied opportunities and their work is often more dangerous during charro cowboy competitions.

In this chapter, I will analyse the socialization process of charro cowboys with generational ties and charro cowboy rookies hoping to be one day accepted by their peers. I will highlight the subtle ways in which lower class charro cowboys with generational ties negotiate their legitimacy with the charro cowboy tradition. The emphasis on "bloodline" as the only true component in "belonging" to the tradition will be the most used defense mechanism among poor and working class charro cowboys. Further, the expression of legitimacy and authentic ties to the community diverge significantly between the younger and older generations of charro cowboys. While the older generation of charro cowboys are more likely to feel that authenticity depends upon generational ties, the younger generation of charro cowboys with generational ties will make an effort to make more inclusive statements about charro cowboy rookies. However, these expressions of inclusivity depend on the audience. Ultimately, I will argue that charro cowboy rookies with indigenous ties experience higher incidents of marginalization and acts of exclusion from generational charro cowboys in their socialization process than generational charro cowboy. This, in conclusion, demonstrates the contradicting notions of the charro cowboy community because the charro cowboy tradition proceeded from indigenous exclusion from Spanish colonial life.

## Charro cowboy socialization, identity, and legitimacy

Although the original charro cowboys were of lower economic background, today charro cowboy men come from diverse socioeconomic backgrounds. Some have even experienced great social and economic mobility in the last three decades. The early charro cowboys of the colonial and post-colonial period in Mexico dedicated their lives to their ranches and animals. Although there were a few wealthy charro cowboys in the early 20th century, most charro cowboys resided in working-class rural areas in Mexico. The notion of the "professional charro cowboy" did not occur until the formal organization of the charro cowboy community in the 1920s due to the growing standardization within the community and the pressure from the Mexican Federation of charro cowboys to expand the audience base of competitions. Those who labeled themselves as a "professional charro cowboy" made their money by participating with teams funded by wealthy charro cowboy *jefes*. Since the charro cowboy tradition is the national sport of Mexico, professional charro cowboys can be regarded as professional athletes without the nationwide notoriety of professional soccer players. Some are recognized within the charro cowboy community but only a few have national or international recognition.[1] However, not every professional charro cowboy is funded by charro cowboy *jefes* and some even find themselves in continuous financial distress due to the growing costs of participating. These professional charro cowboys often have modest ranches that provide them with enough money to support their families and pay their competition and association fees. The source of income varies greatly within the charro cowboy community because they invest a great amount of money in cattle and reigning horses. Many well-known charro cowboys make a living training horses for charro cowboy competitions for their team members or customers from various parts of Mexico and the United States. Nevertheless, there are arguments within the community with respect to who can claim legitimate and authentic status as a charro cowboy.

Generational ties are often the most significant claim to the charro cowboy tradition, regardless of socioeconomic status. Due to the growing importance of wealth in the community, many working class charro cowboys have to rationalize their low socioeconomic status by drawing on their generational ties to enhance their self-worth and identity. This became the greatest attribute for their continuous participation despite always being in debt and not being able to afford the luxuries of other charro cowboy teams. For example, Mario is a 41-year-old charro cowboy with generational ties from a small town outside of Arrandas, Jalisco. His grandfather, Juan, owned a sizable plot of land where they grow crops and tend cattle. Mario's grandfather was a notable charro cowboy in his pueblo, noted for his ability to train even the most stubborn horses. Mario's father, Enrique, inherited the land and continued to grow crops and expand the cattle business. He added another room to his childhood home; however, they did not have modern appliances like a stove, refrigerator, washing machine, etc. Enrique met his wife at the age of 17 during a charro cowboy festival adjacent to his hometown and married her shortly thereafter. Mario is the third of 12 children and all his family consider themselves to be an "authentic charro cowboy family." Mario expressed that although his family did not have much money growing up, they did not need money to be charro cowboys. He stated:

> Look, mi hija, [my daughter], the charro cowboy tradition is for the people who worked hard. During the time of my grandfather, you did not need a ton of… a ton of money. You were a charro cowboy because what you did with your hands. (Gestures to his horse) Those [horses] are the reason you want to do this. My father taught us everything we know and made sure that we were rich in traditions. I see these pendejos (dumbasses) that think money makes them charro cowboys…(laughs). The charro cowboys of the past were like me. Like my family. Don't be fooled by them. It's not true to us (the charro cowboys).
>
> (Interview, May 2013)

Mario's emphasis on the generational connection to the charro cowboy community provides him with a basis to claim charro cowboy identity since he lacks the capital to acquire expensive horses or better equipment. Similar to the inner-directed charro cowboys in the older generation, hard work, expert horsemanship, and family is all one needs to be a "true charro cowboy". Mario recognizes that his lower-socioeconomic position may result in others discrediting his charro cowboy identity and he is quick to shut down such remarks. By reaffirming his generational and familial connections, Mario is able to re-establish his self-worth and identity as an authentic and legitimate charro cowboy.

To further emphasize his claim to the charro cowboy community, Mario and his wife took me to her great grandfather's family home. This area is now abandoned but required a 17-minute ride into the deep swamp of rural Jalisco. The entrance was built with rocks from the surrounding fields and the home was barely standing when I saw it in 2013. The walls were made of brick and a broken wooden door was all that was left to indicate that a family once lived there. Mario's wife told me that there was no plumbing and that her family used to bathe in the river a few meters behind the home. The kitchen had a fire pit and still had a badly rusted metal comal or griddle, once used to heat up tortillas and food. The most important feature of the land was the still standing horse stalls and small training circle. Mario's wife said that these had been built by her grandfather and father. Although the house was in a terrible condition, the stalls and training circle were still in very good shape. Mario and his wife repeatedly expressed that this land, in addition to their own, demonstrated their authentic membership to the charro cowboy community. They were very hostile to any alternative definitions of authenticity.

This type of defense mechanism is not unique to the charro cowboy community. For example, in *The Color of Class: Poor Whites and the Paradox of Privilege* (2003), Kirby Moss examines the how poor whites in the United States negotiate social class and racial category. He reveals the paradoxical nature of whiteness within the bounds of social class. Moss argues:

> Where many scholars draw an unconscious or unrequested racial line between poverty and working class—non-Whites poor and Whites working class (or blue collar, a term many use interchangeably)—my research disrupts by showing that poor Whites exist as a discursive anomaly. A group who, rather than identify or be identified with forms of poverty, identifies instead with forms of privilege because they see themselves in Whiteness and all of its promise. Yet, within that privileged category there are distinct cultural and class differences between poor, working-class, and middle-class White folk that are often glossed over in representations we commonly see linked to poverty and privilege.
>
> (Moss 2003, 22)

Although Moss is examining poor Whites in the Midwest, the use of a privileged category is a fundamental tool of lower class charro cowboys with generational ties. Racial categories in Mexico are not institutionalized as in the United States; however, race relations in the United States can be stratified based on indigenous, mestizo, European lineage, and socio-economic status. In this case, the charro cowboy community as the source of privileged category is authenticity and legitimacy to the charro cowboy tradition. Lower class charro cowboys like Mario are not discriminated in the charro cowboy tradition based on racial or ethnic categorization but rather their social class. My observations of Mario led me to believe that wealthier charro cowboys stigmatized him because of his clothing, horses, etc. based on their subtle comments and their actions of exclusion (i.e. not extending business opportunities to selling livestock or invitations to informal social gatherings). It should also be noted that Mario does not have any markers of indigenous identity such as darker skin color or indigenous traditions. Mario's marginalization from his wealthier charro cowboy peers is based on his class status. Although these actions of exclusion are not always recognized by Mario, he was aware enough of the class differences within the community to use his generational ties as the only form of quintessential charro cowboy legitimacy and authenticity.

This understanding of racial relations allows for the more sharpened framing of Veblen's understanding of the leisure class and its discriminatory practices. In Veblen's introductory chapter of the *Theory of the Leisure Class* (1899), he argued that communities without a defined leisure class often resemble one another in social structure and manners of everyday life. The main components of what he identified as "primitive populations" are peaceable habits in which individual ownership is not the dominant feature of the economic system. In respect to the emergence of the leisure class, Veblen stated:

> The ground on which a discrimination between facts is habitually made changes as the interest from which the facts are habitually viewed changes… The habit of distinguishing and classifying the various purposes and directions of activity prevails of necessity always and everywhere; for it is indispensable in reaching a working theory or scheme of life. The particular point of view, or the particular characteristic that is pitched upon as a definitive in the classification of the facts of life depends upon the interest from which a discrimination of the facts is sought. The grounds of discrimination, and the norm of procedure in classifying the facts, therefore progressively change as the growth of culture proceeds; for the end for which the facts of life are apprehended changes also. So that what are recognised as the salient and decisive features of a class of activities or of a social class at one stage of culture will not retain the same relative importance for the purposes of classification at any subsequent stage.
>
> (Veblen 1899, 5–6)

Social class distinctions are not only based on economic factors in the charro cowboy community, but beyond the ethnic categories that Mexico has struggled to address for generations. The charro cowboy community, due to the continued acceptance of business principles, has opened discrimination based on socially constructed distinctions of the emerging charro cowboy leisure class. Discrimination can seem to be based on differences of socialization. Honorific marks or characteristics that demonstrate proper socialization, as Veblen argued, become the dominant form of distinguishing those who perform hard labor and those who are "well-bred". This process begins in early childhood for many charro cowboys.

Many charro cowboys, whether in the older or younger generation, hold the firm belief that the charro cowboy community is a space in which boys become men. West and Zimmerman's "Doing Gender" (1987) draws attention to gender differences as accomplished through routine social interactions of the everyday. Gender can be divided between the masculine and feminine while its expectations are set by historical, cultural, and institutional contexts. Judith Butler defines gender as "an identity tenuously constituted in time, instituted in an exterior space through a *stylized repetition of acts*" (Butler,

1990). Gender, according to Butler (1990), is a performative accomplishment in which both the social audience and the actors themselves come to believe and to perform its expectations. The charro cowboy tradition stipulates a rural Mexican masculinity that requires constant enactment and negotiation with the historical significance of its past. Gutmann (1996) argued that the conception of masculinity, dominance and power of men over women, has remained fairly consistent in Mexican culture yet Mexican masculinity has expanded its boundaries in the domestic and social roles. Mexican masculinity fits what Connell and Messerschmidt (2005) described as the hegemonic masculine model that identifies multiple masculinities that fluctuate over time, culture, and person. The charro cowboy masculinity is only one component of hegemonic masculinity that allow charro cowboy men to sustain a leading and dominant role in the community through its engagement and active participation with the charro cowboy tradition. Charro cowboy men express a personal responsibility in socializing younger charro cowboys, whether they are their own children or other charro cowboy youngsters, into the tradition and making them "true charro cowboy men".

Kimmel (2008) argues that sports dominated by men have become a space in which men escape and can reinstate their masculinity away from women. Since Mexican dominant society has accepted women into public domains such as business and education, Mexican men often find spaces to express masculinity. Veblen (1899) can further broaden his argument regarding the barbaric and predatory habits to sports and the construction of manhood. He states:

> These manifestations of the predatory temperament are all to be classed under the head of exploit. They are partly simple and unreflected expressions of an attitude of emulative ferocity, partly activities deliberately entered upon with a view to gaining repute for prowess. Sports of all kinds are of the same general character, including prize-fights, bull-fights, athletics, shooting, angling, yachting, and games of skill, even where the element of destructive physical efficiency is not an obtrusive feature.
>
> (Veblen 1899, 117)

Although the charro cowboy tradition has peaceable elements, one cannot deny the predatory and barbaric features that pervade its formal institutionalization as a sport. Participation in sport, according to Veblen, is "essentially of the nature of invidious exploit".

Sport, as argued by Veblen, speaks to the boyish temperament to exploit and conquer. Similar to Kimmel's (2008) argument, sport is a space to freely express masculinity and the charro cowboy tradition is no different. The charro cowboy community provides young charro cowboys with the opportunity to be around other charro cowboy men while also learning the expectation of how to be a charro cowboy man. These spaces are hypermasculine because of the types of conversations that take place. Although the dominant Mexican culture may allude to more egalitarian practices and gender equity, the charro cowboy tradition has become a "safer space" to enact masculinity without the threat of femininity. Charro cowboy men, of any socio-economic class, can engage in conversations with one another without censoring themselves because the charro cowboy community is their domain and women are supplementary. Conversations between charro cowboy men often take the form of informal life lessons that will encourage ideologies that reproduce and reaffirm particular aspects of the charro cowboy tradition.

Further, the assessment of rural masculinity in this context has to be negotiated and protected continuously against urbanity. To better understand this masculinity renegotiation, we can look to the work of Brandt and Haugen's (2005) study of Norway's rural masculinity. The authors examine how rural spaces where agricultural work was the prominent is now experiencing commodification of natural and cultural resources. Rural masculinity in rural spaces is shifting from being expressed through actual agricultural labor to elements of rural activities such as fishing, hunting, and wilderness related activities. In the context of the charro cowboy community, some charro cowboys, in particular the younger ones who reside in urban areas and have a college education, use the charro cowboy competitions as a safe space to enact rural Mexican masculinity without judgment of other non-charro cowboy people. Further, since many of the *charreadas* organized by the Mexican Federation of Charros are in urban areas, the charro cowboy community becomes a rural activity that allows the existence of rural charro cowboy masculinity to continue from generation to generation within these urban spaces. Many charro cowboys perform a form of code switching when they face of other members of the charro cowboy community versus Mexican outsiders. Code switching is common among the younger generation and charro cowboys of high socio-economic status. For most, socialization into the charro cowboy community commences from birth and never truly ends as long as a charro cowboy is always involved in the community through formal or informal organizations of *charreadas*.

The vignette at the beginning of the chapter demonstrates just how early young charro cowboys are socialized into the community by their fathers. Some children can barely walk but they will be mounted on horses, expected to one day participate in the tradition themselves. This socialization is fundamental to the development of their charro cowboy identity and involves continuous interactions with other charro cowboys within the community. These types of observations between sons and fathers are not rare in the charro cowboy community and can be witnessed at any particular *charreada* throughout Mexico and the United States. Gerardo has made sure to expose his son to horses so that he will be less scared to ride them in the future as his father did for him and his brothers. Gerardo Jr. can be considered a very skilled horseman for his early age and many other older charro cowboys say its because it's in his blood. Although he has learned how to handle a horse, Gerardo Jr. has much to learn and is always being told how to act by his father as well as other older charro cowboys.

I observed Gerardo and Gerardo Jr. at several *charreadas* throughout my research. Other older charro cowboys with generational ties would try to advise Gerardo Jr. on the ethics of being a charro cowboy man. In one specific instance, Gerardo Jr. was slouching and his bow, a fundamental piece of the charro cowboy attire, was crooked. One older and more experienced charro cowboy on Gerardo's team grabbed Gerardo Jr.'s arm and told him to sit tall because only "tired old ladies slouch". Another charro cowboy laughed and signaled the young charro cowboy to fix his bow. Gerardo Jr. quickly adjusted himself and continued to smile happily as any happy six-year-old would in the presence of adults. Gerardo Jr. would be continuously monitored for the course of his charro cowboy career.

Pedro, is a 35-year-old charro cowboy with generational ties. He has a ten-year-old son, Marco, from a previous marriage. Because divorce is not very common among charro cowboy families, Pedro's friends and family never mention the fact that his current partner is not his first wife. This shows respect to his current wife and is due to the conservative Roman Catholic beliefs of many of the charro cowboy families. Admitting the divorce would lead to more stigma for charro cowboy women since feminine piety is highly respected and evidence of a second marriage holds the stigma of feminine promiscuity.

Pedro has a total of three children, however, Pedro only has one son or only one true heir to the charro cowboy tradition. This is because charro cowboy men are the visible center point of the charro cowboy tradition (the role of women will be discussed in Chapter 4). The charro cowboy community emphasizes the father and son relationship due to the importance of reproducing the charro cowboy tradition. This is significant to the generational charro cowboys since inculcating the tradition links the young with the old charro cowboy. His relationship with his son is not the most loving compared to the other charro cowboys that I observed due to their particular familial circumstances. Yet, Pedro, like most charro cowboy fathers, does want Marco to be a charro cowboy therefore he is very harsh with his son when it comes to practicing. The following observation depicts Pedro's attempt to instruct his son:

> During a practice session at Pedro's father's ranch in June 2014, Pedro had returned from the opposite end of the mountainside to check up on his children who are riding their horses in the lienzo. He had herded all his cattle and made sure that none of the neighboring ranches had attempted to cross on his land. He was smoking a cigarette as he approached closer to the lienzo. He is an avid chain smoker so it is not rare to see him with a permanent smoke cloud around him. Pedro's father was hosting a practice session for some of his charro cowboy friends and people were beginning to arrive one by one. One truck full of men pulled into the side of the makeshift lienzo and began unloading their equipment. They greeted the children and began setting up the fire pit to make

tacos for everyone. Marco had been playing in the lienzo with his sister and they seemed to be having a good time. He was laughing and yelling out for his sister to race him when he realized his father was approaching. Pedro entered the lienzo and asked Marco to do part of a cala de caballo. Marco's demeanor completely changed from happy to agitated but he did what was asked of him. His suerte involves the charro cowboy sprinting from his horse the 90-meter mark of the lienzo and then making a sudden stop at the 50-meter line leading the horse to glide the back of its legs potentially across a 15-meter mark. The smoother the glide and the longer the distance, the more a charro cowboy is able to demonstrate that the he has excellent control and domination of his horse. Since this a practice session, there are no judges and there are no restrictions about movement. Pedro has been teaching his son how to do this particular suerte since he was five years old. Since the purpose of the cala de caballo is to demonstrate a charro cowboy's horsemanship skills, this particular suerte often takes years to perfect. Marco, reluctantly, struts his horse to the 90-meter mark and proceeded to sprint the horse to the 50-meter mark. The men on the outside of the lienzo were attentively watching the young boy as he proceeded to attempt the cala de caballo. Marco was able to slide the horse at a sizable distance but was noticeably scared when the horse's legs struggled to balance. He had not controlled the horse well enough and the horse had jumped slightly from the sand. The other charro cowboys watching were impressed however Pedro was not. He gave Marco little praise and proceeded to tell him all the movements that he had done wrong. He exclaimed, "Don't look nervous! Do you ever see me nervous? No. A charro cowboy has to be ready and calm." Marco quietly agreed and said that he would do better. Pedro asked Marco to repeat the cala de caballo until he felt that Marco was at the standard that he wanted him to be. At Marco's final attempt, Pedro finally praised him and Marco waited until his father wasn't looking to shed a tear.

(Observation, 2014)

Although Pedro and Marco's father-son relationship is marred by external familial problems, Pedro's responsibility as a charro cowboy father is to teach his son about their tradition. Pedro has been criticised by other charro cowboys for not dedicating enough time to teaching his son. Pedro's close friend has mentioned that he is not sure why Pedro does not dedicate enough time to his son since a lot of charro cowboys with daughters wish they had a son to teach. The *cala de caballo* is one of the most difficult *suertes* because of the technical precision that is required of the charro cowboy therefore requires extensive practice. Mastering the *cala de caballo* takes many years therefore the manner in which Pedro pressures his son is not uncommon and often the norm for many charro cowboy families.

Manuel, 25 years old, is also a charro cowboy with three generational ties to the charro cowboy community. Originally from Guanajuato, Manuel now lives on the outskirts of Guadalajara on the ranch that his charro cowboy *jefe* owns. When recalling his childhood, Manuel focuses on his charro cowboy upbringing and his relationship with his father. Although his mother was a stay-at-home mom, Manuel rarely mentions her in his stories about his childhood. He centered his stories around how his father taught him to be the charro cowboy that he is today. It was interesting to see how he associated his father with his most recent achievements. He said the following:

> When I was 12, my father had just traded some horses to a neighbor for some bulls. These bulls were... giant. Bad tempered, big balled, assholes. (laughs) [My father] was very happy about [this trade] because we wanted to show me how to ride the bull (jineto el toro) on bigger bulls... I had only tried it on smaller bulls before (laughs). You don't break your face on the nice ones. I was very stubborn though and would say that I didn't want to learn. He could tell that I was nervous...but he wouldn't let me do anything else until I would get on the bull. One day... I got on the bull but he poked it so hard with a stick that I almost fell off from the buck. I was so scared because I thought that I was going to hit my head on the metal bar. I had already broken a rib the previous year so I was more nervous than I should have been. My father just laughed and yelled at me to hold on tighter and adjust my legs and posture. He is one of the best bull riders of his generation so I am glad he was my teacher. If he didn't threat to kick my ass if I fell, I would probably be terrible.
>
> (Interview, 2013)

Manuel is currently one of the best bull riders in Mexico. He also wishes to teach his future sons the charro cowboy tradition when the time comes for him to start a family. He has a girlfriend who frequently mentions being from a charro cowboy family and he plans to get more serious with her in coming years. In his interview, he described being physically reprimanded by his father if he did not succeed in a *suerte*, whether in practice or competition. Although Manuel is a part of the younger generation of charro cowboys, he shares the experiences of the older generation of charro cowboys when it comes to training and socialization in the charro cowboy community. The memories he shares, in his opinion, do not reflect an almost abusive relationship, but rather a romanticized understanding of the past.

The romanticized past did not become evident until later. During one of my competition observations of Manuel, his cousin, Yessica was there with her husband who is also a charro cowboy for another charro cowboy *jefe*. Manuel would frequently explain relationships within the community that I was not familiar with in order to understand why some people did not talk to each other. It was not common for me to overhear Manuel talking to other people. In 2013, weeks after Manuel's first formal interview with me, a man who Manuel knew from high school came up to him to catch up. His cousin Yessica was next to me, and she also knew this man. The man asked Manuel how his father was doing and Yessica started giggling next to me. Manuel glared at her, but continued to say that his father was fine. Yessica whispered in my ear, "Manuel hates that man", as in his father. I was surprised to hear this and Manuel later told me that he resented his father for always pressuring him. He stated, "He almost got me killed because he wanted more from me."

Angel is a 70-year-old charro cowboy from Mexico City and like Manuel, his father was also ruthless about his charro cowboy lessons. Angel recalls various times when his father was violent toward him if did not successfully achieve a *suerte* when he was younger. Older charro cowboys were more comfortable sharing stories of violent episodes with their fathers than the younger charro cowboys. He also narrated these incidents in the similar romantic tone as Manuel. Most of the charro cowboys that recalled harsh reprimands from their fathers did not view these incidents as child abuse. Although not every charro cowboy in the community experienced any form of physical abuse, the charro cowboy respondents that I interviewed tended to imply that physical punishment is a common tool of discipline. These charro cowboys viewed these incidents as necessary to establish their dedication in the charro cowboy tradition.

These violent episodes are evidence of the consequences of the barbaric and predatory cultural habits that are embedded within the charro cowboy community. It was not rare within families for the father to compare the skill of one brother with another. This was certainly the case for brothers Memo, 39, and Santos, 37. These brothers shared the same background of many charro cowboy families and were fierce competitors. The brothers had an extensive rivalry that had been introduced by their father. Although Santos was the younger brother, he was the most successful and talented. Santos recalled moments in his upbringing when his father would yell at his older brother, Memo, for failing to meet his expectations. Memo resented this, but nevertheless, continued to compete separately with his uncles and cousins. During Memo's interview, he explained:

> My father is a hard man. He would never be happy with how I was holding the reigns or even how I was mounting it. He really paid attention to [Santos]...he was the more talented one. But my father made me better than I was... I remember one day I fell off the horse because the saddle was not on tight enough. I must have been ten or eleven at the time... (laughs)... he took me by the hair because I refused to get on the horse. He made me watch my brother [Santos] calar [cala de caballo] until the sun went down. He yelled to me, "Watch and learn!" I was angry but I never let him see me fall again.
>
> (Interview, 2013)

Although Memo had a difficult relationship with his father, he was still able to romanticize his relationship with his father. Santos also described similar moments of violence and forcefulness by his father. Memo and Santos were always compared to one another, limiting their brotherly bond. At the time that I observed and interviewed them, they had limited communication with one another and had a history of not talking for years.

Veblen would describe the violent elements of the charro cowboy's childhood past as a consequence of the predatory phase of life. The charro cowboy father is presented with the responsibility of socializing his child into the tradition, yet he surpasses peaceably savagery when he engages in exploitation. Veblen argued:

> The activity of the men more and more takes on the character of exploit; and an invidious comparison of one hunter or warrior with another continually easier and more habitual. Tangible evidences of prowess—trophies—find a place in men's habits of thought as an essential feature of the paraphernalia life. Booty, trophies of the chase or the raid, come to be prized as evidence of preeminent force. Aggression becomes the accredited form of action, and booty serves as prima facie evidence of successful aggression.
>
> (Veblen 1899, 9)

The invidious comparison is a common result of these social dynamics presented in socialization, however, through further analysis, we will see that they are exacerbated as trophies become more valuable in the charro cowboy community.

The socialization into the charro cowboy community is often, as previously mentioned, a group effort among the older generation of charro cowboys. It is noteworthy to mention that this extension of help or charro cowboy wisdom is only granted to young charro cowboys with generational ties because there is a sense of personal responsibility in keeping the tradition alive. The older generation with generational ties will not necessarily seek out young charro cowboys to mentor. However, these types of relationships occur more organically between generational charro cowboys because there are ample opportunities for mentorship to occur. As mentioned earlier, the older generation of charro cowboys often hosts informal *charreadas* to spend time with other charro cowboys. Sometimes, generational charro cowboys will bring their young children to practices and older charro cowboys will take these opportunities to teach the young charro cowboys skills. Although the trajectory of what the charro cowboy identity represents and embodies depends on generational lines, young charro cowboys with generational ties have a deep respect for older charro cowboys.

When asked, many charro cowboys will reference their own family members and family friends as being inspirational, serving as the baseline for their future goals. For example, Martín, a 20-year old charro cowboy with generational ties, stated that he idolizes the older generation of charro cowboys for their skills and ideas regarding charro cowboy brotherhood. Although Martín has characteristics that would classify him as other-directed, he highlighted the significance of mentorship between the older charro cowboys and young charro cowboys because that was the basis of the charro cowboy tradition. He stated:

> My grandfather and father are my biggest mentors. They have made me the charro cowboy that I am today. Everything that I do…I do because I learned from them. They always give me advice…even when I do not want to hear it (laughs). They taught me that one must be disciplined to be in this. Train a minimum of three times a week if you to be in competitions. I think you have to have a strong character to be a charro cowboy and that is what my father taught me.
>
> (Interview, August 2013)

Martín credits his father and grandfather for his charro cowboy character. His socialization began as a child and continued into his early adulthood.

The purpose of training one charro cowboy generation is to bestow and reproduce a specific type of charro cowboy manhood while refining their charro cowboy horsemanship skills. As stated previously, the charro cowboy tradition has been formally institutionalized as the official sport of Mexico and as a result, the tradition has some sport-like characteristics, which is how it mostly thrives in Mexico. Incidentally, this is also true of the charro cowboy sportsmanship in *charreadas*. While the Mexican Federation of Charros judge vigilantly charro cowboy horsemanship, portions of the Official and General Rules for Competitions 2012–2016 also evaluate charro cowboy sportsmanship and points can be deducted based on the lack of appropriate temperament. Evaluation of charro cowboy sportsmanship is not a new incorporation to the rules like the strict measurement of distance or time. Charro cowboy sportsmanship is significant to the tradition since the original purpose of *charreadas* was to celebrate the tradition with adjacent rural pueblos.

Charro cowboy fathers training their sons will often teach their children about sportsmanship in the charro cowboy tradition. As stated earlier, charro cowboys believe in the welfare of animals and often chastise charro cowboys who injury their horses. Charro cowboy children are taught from a young age to never hit their horses and if they there can be serious consequences. For example, Jorge, a 16-year-old charro was practicing with his father, Torbio on a Sunday afternoon in July 2015. My associations with Jorge were intertwined with his father, Torbio who had invited me to his ranch to observe his everyday work. Jorge had been trying to perfect his *cala de caballo*. The horse was becoming aggravated by the continuous practice and Torbio noticed. Torbio yelled at his son to bring the horse in for rest and continue in an hour. Jorge, looking tired, agreed. However, he yelled back that he wanted to try the *cala* run one more time. His father reluctantly agreed but allowed him to continue. Jorge's horse sprinted across the 90-meter mark but halted abruptly as it reached the 50-meter mark. Jorge was noticeably irate and began yelling at his horse and grabbed his whip to punish the horse. Torbio looked noticeably angry and told his son loudly to drop the whip and go home. Jorge did exactly what his father asked and proceeded to walk toward the other end of the *lienzo*. Jorge looked scared, knowing that he was going to be punished in private. Torbio apologized to me for losing his temper in front of a woman.[2] He made a point of telling me that he wanted to prevent his son from becoming someone who does not respect the "horses that feed him." Torbio was implying that the horses in his ranch provide him with capital to take care of his family. He further added that the charro cowboy tradition is about respecting the horse since they are what gave their ancestors freedom from the Spanish.

Charro cowboy teenagers with generational ties are even more monitored and regulated by charro cowboy men with generational ties. In particular, older charro cowboy men will frequently engage in conversations with adolescent charro cowboy boys in order to make sure that they are being correctly conditioned to the tradition. Many young adolescent charro cowboys admire their older charro cowboy counterparts for their skills but others esteem their wealth and honor more. Either way, adolescent charro cowboys will respect the authority of older charro cowboys with generational ties and will adhere to their expectations. This is not because they necessarily want to, but because they will be faced with overwhelming pressure through force or public embarrassment if they don't adhere to the older charro cowboy's expectations. In a particular incident in June 2013, an older charro cowboy with generational ties was drinking tequila and coke near the entrance to the audience. A young charro cowboy aged about 17 walked toward the older charro cowboy to greet him. The older charro cowboy grabbed the young charro cowboy by the shoulder and proceeded to exclaim his excitement to see him. The older charro cowboy offered him a drink but the young charro cowboy rejected his offer with a slight smile. Annoyed, the older charro cowboy proceeded to pour him a shot of tequila anyway. He stated:

> Mi hijo [my son] …a charro cowboy never turns down tequila (laughs). Here, take this. Now take the shot and never make a face. If you do, everyone is going to think you are weak. A Mexican takes his drink forcefully. (hands the young charro cowboy his drink) Now take it. Drink it! Act like you like it! (laughs) He watched him carefully, waiting for the young teenager to do exactly what he wanted.

Having no choice, the young charro cowboy took his shot and tries not to make a face. Despite his best efforts, the young charro cowboy let out a gasp and reached out for a drink of soda that the older charro cowboy handed him, laughing at the sight of the struggling young charro cowboy.

I witnessed countless teenage charro cowboys drink at the demand of their older charro cowboy counterparts. Although Mexico's drinking age is 18, it was not uncommon to see underage charro cowboys drink heavily at competitions. In the summer of 2013, I observed a ten-year-old boy holding his own *michelada*, a spicy Mexican beer and lime cocktail, while watching the *coleadero*. His father was watching his father compete and one of his older cousins was also drinking. The older cousin, an older teenager, called the boy by his nickname, "Michelada" to attract his attention to the group of rowdy charro cowboys in front of them. He told the boy loudly, "See that's what happens when you drink too much. You have to learn to hold your liquor or you will be rodeo clowns like them [referring to the very drunk charro cowboy in front of them]. The boy smiled and stated, 'I know. I am charro [cowboy] like my dad.'" Throughout my research, I observed various times when Michelada would drink openly in front of his parents. He would only be allowed one drink but the boy was always proud to feel like he was being included in the group of older charro cowboy men.

Alcohol consumption in the charro cowboy community is a common practice and is encouraged, becoming another socialization tool similar to the way that young boys are told how to sit or act at *charreadas*. Veblen states, "Drunkenness and the other pathological consequences of the free use of stimulants therefore tend in their turn to become honorific, as being a mark, at the second remove, of the superior status of those who are able to afford the indulgence" (Veblen 1899, 34). In the charro cowboy community, alcohol is a tool in the expression of the charro cowboy community's particular rural masculinity and drinking is an honorific act, only if done in a particular manner. While not every charro cowboy engages in drunken behavior, many recognize its significance to the process of becoming an authentic and legitimate charro cowboy. Some charro cowboys with generational ties recognize that alcoholism runs in their family but attribute these alcoholic tendencies as minimal and easily contained. I observed many young adolescent charro cowboys watching older charro cowboys drink and even in some cases mimic the behaviors of their idols. To an 18-year-old charro cowboy that I interviewed, drinking alcohol to him is just a form of charro cowboy expression that they have learned from watching the older generation of charro cowboys. Drinking tequila at a *charreada* is viewed as an expression of cultural identity.

Veblen stated, "In popular apprehension there is much that is admirable in the type of manhood which the life of sport fosters. There is self-reliance and good-fellowship, so termed in the some-what loose colloquial use of the words" (Veblen 1899, 120). The notion of self-reliance and fellowship is also central to the charro cowboy tradition because it is a peaceable trait that requires the nurturing of relationships with others. However, sportsmanship is transformed into a barbaric or predatory practice once exploitation of the other or even the individual occurs. Further, Veblen stated, "The physical vigor acquired in the training for athletic games—so far as the training may be said to have this effect—is of advantage both to the individual and the collectivity, serviceability. The spiritual traits which go with athletic sport are likewise economically advantageous to the individual, as contradistinguished from the interests of the collectivity" (Veblen 1899, 120). The charro cowboy training is beneficial for the individual's cultivation of their skills and their place in the charro cowboy community. The collective interests of the charro cowboy community are also met since the tradition is being replicated from one generation to another.

The notion of "good sportsmanship" is central to the charro cowboy tradition, nevertheless "good sportsmanship" varies in the charro cowboy community. The generational charro cowboys tend to be pleasant to other generational charro cowboys though unfriendly to charro cowboy rookies. The younger generation of charro cowboys with generational ties are more devious with their sportsmanship towards rookies since they have a more other-directed social character. Their other-directed social character, as Riesman argued, demands that their answer does not differ from the rest of the group. Since the younger generation of charro cowboys with generational ties want to be liked and seem like they are receptive to newcomers in the community, their responses will reflect notions of free opportunity rather than exclusion. Riesman stated, "The thoroughly other-directed the individual is, the more unhesitatingly able he is to classify his preferences and to compare those of others. In fact, as compared with their inner-directed predecessors, other-directed children are extraordinarily knowledgeable about popularity rating" (Riesman 1961, 81). The other-directed charro cowboy is also able to formulate his responses to the standards of newcomers, giving the illusion that they are not exclusionary with regards to charro cowboy rookies.

For example, when asked if anyone could be a charro cowboy, about 36 out 42 of the charro cowboys between the ages of 18 to 35 with generational ties said that any person had the right to become a charro cowboy if they showed true passion. Gustavo, the 25-year-old charro cowboy with generational ties, mentioned previously explaining:

> If they like…and they like it a lot…I think that if they go meet the right people at competitions that are bosses of teams maybe they can find a place to ride. Dedication, education, and attitude. It's the only thing [they] need. Who am I to judge… if they want to compete. Not everyone thinks like me… but who knows… (nervous laughs).
>
> (Interview, July 2014)

Gustavo's charro cowboy team is a mixture of generational charro cowboys and charro cowboy rookies. His closest friend on the team is a charro cowboy rookie from rural village in Mexico, however in the three years that I got to know Gustavo, he revealed that some charro cowboys are better than others in subtle ways. When a charro cowboy with generational ties did not continuously perform well, he would make comments regarding his bloodlines. He would say, "It's in their blood. They will get better", while Gustavo would not justify lack of skill in charro cowboy rookies. His comments were coded to not appear exclusive to other charro cowboy rookies and to promote his well-liked persona.

Gustavo wanted to avoid the stereotype that charro cowboys can be racist and classist against marginalized ethnic groups in Mexico. During one of our interviews, Gustavo stated that he really resented the fact that charro cowboys were stereotyped as drunks, womanizers, and racists. He stated, "Some are but those [charro cowboys] don't represent all of us." Gustavo was referring to charro cowboys who distinguish themselves by invidious discrimination. Veblen would characterize this as the separation of the noble and ignoble classes that is characteristic of predatory and barbaric habits in society. Although Gustavo attempted to be more accepting of newcomers, his socialization could not be avoided. Even his own family members said that the charro cowboy had skills that were only passed down by blood.

Joel, a 22-year-old charro cowboy with generational ties, answered the question, "Can any person become a charro cowboy and compete in *charreadas*?" in a similar way to Gustavo. In his interview, Joel made sure to let me know that he believed that any man could become a charro cowboy if they put enough work into it. Joel is from a wealthy family therefore he knows a fair amount of charro cowboy rookies that have gained access into the community through financial means. However, like Gustavo, Joel also made similar comments that suggested that charro cowboys with generational ties have more claim to the tradition. Joel's other-directed social character prevents him from deviating from the peer-group, in this case being in the younger generation of charro cowboys. For example, during a regional competition in Jalisco, Joel was sitting on a metal bar on the edge of the *lienzo* with a few of his charro cowboy teammates. They were observing the *piales en la manga del lienzo* that tends to be performed by the older generation of charro cowboys due to the amount of strength and practice this *suerte* requires. An older charro cowboy, about 60 years old, had correctly and successfully carried out the *pial*. The charro cowboy stopped the sprinting mare with ease before the 90-meter mark. There was moderate cloud of smoke from the friction of the rope and the horn of the saddle. Joel was very impressed by the maneuvering of the older charro cowboy and nudged his friends. He said:

> This grand charro cowboy knows exactly what to do. He does not hesitate or stutter his actions. You don't see that amount of grace in competitions anymore. You can tell that he was meant to be on that horse. It's in his blood. You can't learn that…(laughs) He is a boss. Tell me if you can learn that… because next to him, I complete shit (laughs)!

His friends laugh and continue to make fun of Joel. Gabriel, 20 years old with no generational ties, had aspirations to become a *pialador* and Joel's comments visibly upset him. Joel's other-directed character requires peer approval therefore Joel backtracked his comments by saying, "Maybe you could learn his [Charro cowboy] grace" in order to re-establish his persona as a welcoming charro cowboy and be liked by his team members. He defused the potential source of tension by inviting his charro cowboy team-mates to share a shot of tequila. This was not the first time that Joel had reverted to his nonexclusive statements.

Joel's behavior is indicative of the other-directed social character of the younger generation of charro cowboys. Riesman states, "While all people want and need to be liked by some of the people some of the time, it is only the modern other-directed types who make this their chief source of direction and chief area of sensitivity" (Riesman, 1961). Joel exhibits this other-directed sensitivity and therefore, adjusts his statements around charro cowboy rookies in order to secure their friendship. This type of behavior is not representative of the older generation of charro cowboys. Since their social character is more inner-directed, the older generation of charro cowboys do not mind potentially offending people. Their comments are harsher and they tend be more brutally honest. Riesman described an inner-directed child in the following way:

> Returning now to the situation of the inner-directed child, we see that he finds his playmates either among his own brothers and sisters or in an equally wide age range outside the home. This pattern still exists in rural areas, where the gang at the swimming hole or ball field will be widely ranged in age; there are no partitioned playgrounds. However, after age of "social discretion" is reached, the inner-directed child is expected to confine his friendships to those of approximately his own social class.
>
> (Riesman 1961, 68)

Although the older generation of charro cowboys are beyond their childhood years, the inner-directed modes of friendship still apply. Many of the older generation of charro cowboys only associate or would characterize their friends as other generational charro cowboys. Unlike the younger generation of charro cowboys who tend to have charro cowboy rookies as friends, the older generation of charro cowboys confine their friendships within the bounds of the charro cowboy community that has legitimate generational ties. This difference in friendship marks the differences in upbringing between the older and younger generations of charro cowboys. While some younger charro cowboys grew up in small pueblos in rural Mexico, their active participation in the charro cowboy community exposes them to non-genera-tional charro cowboys and charro cowboys of different socio-economic back-grounds. Their non-generational charro cowboy friends are often their age, meaning that charro cowboy rookies often leave the charro cowboy commu-nity as they get older. The older charro cowboys have set their networks and friendships based on who they grew up with and will gravitate to the same group of friends during each *charreada*. Generally, the older generation of charro cowboys tend to befriend charro cowboys of the same socio-economic class and generational ties. Invidious discrimination is a powerful tool to marginalize non-generational charro cowboys in the community.

For example, a previously identified inner-directed charro cowboy, Samuel's charro cowboy friends are very selective about whom they offer drinks to while making commentating on the *charreada*. His friends are also other generational charro cowboys and they often spent *charreadas* drinking and laughing. The symbol of friendship to Samuel, and to other charro cowboys, is the offering of tequila to another fellow charro cowboy. During one particular *charreada*, Samuel and his friend, Arturo were drinking tequila and discussing the competition. Five shots into their discussion, Arturo pointed to a charro cowboy rookie trying to compete in *el coleadero* or *colas en el lienzo*. The young charro cowboy was barely 18 years old and had only officially competed in the *colas en el lienzo* a couple of times. Arturo, mildly tipsy, told Samuel that the charro cowboy rookie was garbage. "He is new. You can tell." Samuel, pouring tequila into his coke, laughed in agreement. The competitor after the charro cowboy rookie was the son of their great friend and was only a few years younger than the charro cowboy rookie. Samuel said, "Now [gesturing to the charro cowboy] is a real charro cowboy. It is in his blood. It is in his blood. You can tell just by how he positions himself." Arturo carefully examined the generational charro cowboy's actions and said "That's right!"

Samuel and Arturo are not the only charro cowboys in the older generation to use words like "garbage" to describe charro cowboy rookies. Even if the charro cowboy rookie was considered to be a great charro cowboy by his peers or charro cowboy *jefes*, many charro cowboys like Samuel and Arturo reject their success and always find something to criticize. In the same situation, the charro cowboy rookie that they were criticizing had successful enacted the *colas en el lienzo* in his third and final attempt while the generational charro cowboy did not. Rather than praising the charro cowboy rookie, Samuel grabbed his drink and said, "So he can pray...(laughs)." Samuel was highlighting the charro cowboy rookie's luck rather than his skills. Unlike the other-directed charro cowboys whose main focus in conversation is to be liked by others, the inner-directed charro cowboys use their moments of conversation during *charreadas* to unwind and de-stress.

While harsh comments are generally aimed from an older charro cowboy to another, this does not deter them from stating them in front of charro cowboy rookies. While an other-directed charro cowboy would alter their responses in order to not offend other charro cowboy rookies, the inner-directed charro cowboy does not care much about "hurting" or offending charro cowboy rookies. As stated previously, some charro cowboy teams comprise different charro cowboys of different generational backgrounds. Therefore, the older generation of charro cowboy have some personal interactions with charro cowboy rookies. In a particular *charreada*, Rafael (a 63-year-old charro cowboy with generational ties) was drinking coke and tequila with his three of his other charro cowboy friends. Mateo (40 years old), Rafael's son, had asked Rafael to compete with his team because one of his teammates was injured. Rafael was discussing with his friends what he thought about Mateo's team. He said, "There are good ones [charro cowboy] but there is a bunch of garbage." His charro cowboy friends proceeded to laugh. Rafael did not notice that behind him was a group of charro cowboy rookies taking shots with their girlfriends. One of the charro cowboy rookies looked visibly upset. Later on the same night, the charro cowboy rookie went up to Rafael and said, "Am I garbage, Don Rafael?" Rafael was drunk at this point, however, he did not miss a beat and stated, "Pure garbage" while proceeding to laugh. The charro cowboy rookie laughed awkwardly but did not challenge his answer. He instead left the group with his head down.

The older generation of charro cowboy does not identify this type of behavior as mean or even discriminatory. Their ideas regarding ownership of the charro cowboy identity are based on generational ties. Although their younger generational counterparts share similar sentiments about charro cowboy legitimacy, the younger and other-directed charro cowboys will adjust their comments based on their peer group. Nonetheless, the charro cowboy rookies recognize the resistance of the older generation of charro cowboys and the false sincerity of the younger generation of charro cowboys. The instinct of workmanship and their genuinely peaceable motivations are not considered, therefore, the charro cowboy community becomes a toxic space for them. Many charro cowboy rookies end up abandoning the charro cowboy tradition for the American rodeo. Only a select few remain in the tradition for years, solidifying their place so their children can gain eventual generational status.

## Charro cowboy rookies and the charro cowboy community

Charro cowboy *jefes* spend a lot of money recruiting members of their teams. As stated earlier, the charro cowboy *jefes* are interested in acquiring money, prestige, and power within the charro cowboy community. While some charro cowboy *jefes* have a generational tie to the community, many charro cowboy *jefes* have revealed that their interest in the community was the first in their family. Charro cowboy teams comprise charro cowboys with different socio-economic backgrounds and generational ties. This is a great contrast from teams compromised solely of family members or other members of the pueblo community. Charro cowboy *jefes* often recruit aspiring charro cowboys from the very villages that their ranches occupy. Aspiring charro cowboys are usually young ranch hands hired from the local villages that are often brought to *charreadas* to tend to the animals once the charro cowboy has finished competing. These young workers are often underage, poor, and undereducated and see the charro cowboy community as a potential route to elevated social status.

For example, Vicente is a 20-year-old charro cowboy rookie who has been working for his charro cowboy *jefe* since he was 14 years old. Vicente had always admired the charro cowboy tradition but had no generational ties to it. He had grown up watching Pedro Infante films as a kid and watching the charro cowboys sing their love ballads on television. He witnessed how the town's residents admired the charro cowboys in their clean charro cowboy attire and their beautifully decorated sombreros. His family is very poor and they rely on Vicente and his brother for income since his mother is very sick and his father is an alcoholic. His mother identifies herself as indigenous and still speaks her native language. His charro cowboy *jefe* hired Vicente for a low wage however he has grown very fond of him over the years. Because Vicente's father is an alcoholic and has not been a good father to him, Vicente considers his charro cowboy *jefe* to be like a father. Vicente's experience is not generalizable to all charro cowboy rookies but highlights some important experiences that many charro cowboy rookies share.

As a hired ranch hand, Vicente was able to travel with the team throughout different parts of Mexico while observing the very best charro cowboys of the nation. When he was 17, he made the decision that he also wanted to be a charro cowboy and began saving his money for his sombrero, a significant emblem of the charro cowboy tradition. His family was resistant at first since they did not have the money to fund Vicente's dream. Since Vicente is responsible for herding cows on the ranch, he used these opportunities to perfect his charro cowboy skills. Interestingly enough, Vicente practiced his skills very much like the original charro cowboys of the colonial period. Once he had been riding for a few years, he befriended another charro cowboy, Enrique (25 years old with generational ties) who has taught him how to *jinetar* or ride a bull. Many charro cowboy rookies take up bull riding because it requires less investment of time to learn and there are always openings on teams for willing participants. Further, less material and equipment is required compared to other *suertes* such as special ropes or charro cowboy saddles. Although there is less monetary risk, *jinetado* bulls or horses do leave these charro cowboy rookies vulnerable to injury, ranging from rope burns on their hands to critical back injuries. Charro cowboy rookies must have a lot of courage and determination. Many charro cowboy *jefes* recruit young charro cowboy rookies for the *jineto de toro* and the *jineto de yegua* because charro cowboy rookies are more likely to risk injury in the pursuit of honor and acceptance. These *suertes* are also less prestigious and have the most turnaround. Nonetheless, charro cowboy rookies view these *suertes* as an entrance into the community and are willing to put their lives on the line for the opportunity to gain honor and prestige.

Vicente has suffered from various injuries trying to learn the *jineto de toro* but he has been lucky that he heals quickly. Vicente competed in his very first professional charro cowboy competition aged 19. His charro cowboy *jefe* needed a replacement for the *jineto de toro* because the last charro cowboy rookie had broken his leg when a bull stepped on his tibia. Vicente describes his first experience as the following:

> I was so nervous but I was ready. Enrique told me to never let them [other charro cowboy] see me without the charro [cowboy] outfit. He said that I could get confused as a worker. That day was so scary but I knew I wanted this for a long time. I got on that bull and lasted enough to pulled the back rope…. I was nervous so my dismount…my dismount could have been better (laughs).
>
> (Interview, 2015)

Vicente, unlike other charro cowboys with generational ties, was more likely to report incidents of discrimination during *charreadas* than his charro cowboy counterparts. For example, Vicente recalls moments when a drunk, older and experienced charro cowboy called him garbage after his ride because he had beat his nephew in the final scoring results. Other charro cowboys, both young and old with generational ties are less likely to talk to him on the side lines therefore he makes sure to hangout with other charro cowboy rookies with the same socio-economic backgrounds. They often share stories regarding discrimination, allowing them to bond while they relieve stress.

Discrimination in the charro cowboy community is often not discussed because acknowledging it contradicts the foundational charro cowboy ethos of brotherhood. Therefore, there is an illusion of achieved brotherhood that does not exclude others and centeres on the continuity of charro cowboy tradition. Exclusion would be a direct contradiction of the ethos of the charro cowboy tradition that originated from continuous marginalization of mestizo and indigenous Mexicans. The Mexican Federation of Charros has been recorded stating that discrimination in the charro cowboy community is minimal and not accepted. Acknowledging any form of discrimination would counteract the very ethos of the charro cowboy tradition and would break the illusion that the community fundamentally believes in its origins. Attributable to the imagery that the charro cowboy tradition symbolizes, many charro cowboys believe that their tradition is a space in which no change is necessary but rather mainstream Mexican culture is the source of problems of discrimination. Although Jean Baudrillard's *America* (1989) is written in the context of American culture, his theoretical standpoint regarding the "utopia achieved" can be applied to the charro cowboy community. According to Baudrillard (1989), the idea of "utopia achieved" is centered on the fact that America has already conquered racism, sexism, classism, etc. and no real substantive change is necessary. This same concept can be attributed to the charro cowboy tradition. As a result of Mexican independence and various Mexican revolutions, the charro cowboy community is not the source of discrimination because to many generational charro cowboys, these issues have already been conquered or addressed. The charro cowboy community, in particular charro cowboy men, do not see issues of sexism in the community because charro cowboy women fought alongside charro cowboy men during times of war and also have a tradition of their very own.

Many charro cowboy men, specifically charro cowboy men with generational ties, believe the community to be like Baudrillard's "utopia achieved". When I asked older and experienced charro cowboys about discrimination with the community, many were baffled by the question and firmly stated that no problems existed in the "true" charro cowboy community. Every one of the 52 charro cowboys with generational ties that I interviewed was asked about discrimination within the charro cowboy community. Their answers were all the same: "There are no problems." Those few who did mention any form of discrimination only cited class-based distinctions but were hesitant to state any other forms of discrimination such as sexism or colorism. One high-class charro cowboy rookie with no indigenous markers mentioned sexism as a possible form of discrimination and framed his answer with Mexican machismo. Due to this appeal to the charro cowboy illusion of brotherhood, charro cowboy rookies, especially lower class and indigenous charro cowboy rookies, have a harder time coping with discrimination because acknowledging discrimination would lead to their continuous marginalization.

This intrinsic form of discrimination can be framed as a part of what Veblen described as the canons of taste. Canons of taste referred specifically to the leisure class consumption of what was deemed beautiful and valued in its community. This particular theorization can be extended to the participants of the charro cowboy tradition because of the way that preference is given to lighter skinned Mexicans and wealthy families. The charro cowboy culture is consumed and enacted by its participations, in order to ensure its continuity. The illusion of a utopian tradition without any form of marginalization is a tactic to minimize the real and problematic mechanisms of intolerance against newcomers. The discrimination of charro rookies demonstrates how the generational charro cowboy is conditioned to associate the tradition with lighter skinned Mexicans and rural families. Veblen stated:

> Our higher appreciation of the superior article is an appreciation of its superior honorific character, much more frequently than it is an unsophisticated appreciation of its beauty. The requirement of conspicuous wastefulness is not commonly present, consciously, in our canons of taste, but it is none the less present as a constraining norm selectively shaping and sustaining our sense of what is beautiful, and guiding our discrimination with respect to what legitimately be approved as beautiful and what may not.
>
> (Veblen 1899, 60)

Here Veblen's argument pertained to products, yet his case is germane to the understanding of distinctions in the charro cowboy community. Superior honorific character is embedded within the identity of the charro cowboy and generational charro cowboys utilize this aspect to exclude those that do not fit within this paradigm. The charro cowboy identity becomes a possession that is monopolized by those with generational ties, comparable to a possession that generates pride to the individuals that use it. The charro cowboy tradition, for many, has become more about the identity than the original survivors of rural life. The charro cowboy rookie may reflect peaceable and useful attributes, nevertheless, the charro cowboy exclusivity, generated by the canons of taste, produces ownership of authenticity and legitimacy.

Vicente's friend, Mere, is 22-year-old charro cowboy with no generational ties. Like Vicente, Mere comes from a lower socio-economic background and has indigenous ties. He is of a darker complexion and is shorter than the rest of the charro cowboys that he works with on a regular basis. Mere also competes in *charreadas* and does the *jineto de toro*. Unlike his other team members, Mere is not paid to participate in *charreadas* because he owes money to his charro cowboy *jefe* for his equipment. He lives on the ranch and wakes up early to take care of the horses and livestock with another young aspiring charro cowboy. His only source of income comes from doing special jobs for other charro cowboys such as taking care of their horses when they are away or washing their equipment. Although Mere is presented with the illusion that he is on the team, he is not treated as an equal. Often, he overhears other charro cowboys referring to him as the *indio charro* (indigenous charro cowboy) because of his family background. Ironically enough, the very discrimination based on indigenous ties among modern charro cowboys was the very reason why the charro cowboy culture formed in the colonial period. Only the majority of rookie charro cowboys with indigenous ties see these contradictions.

Vicente's indigenous background is not the only basis of his marginalization. Since he grew up outside of the bounds of the charro cowboy tradition, he does not possess the cultural capital that could identify him as a charro cowboy. For example, he lacks some of the greeting rituals and some of the charro cowboy terms that are widely used by generational charro cowboys. Since some charro cowboys with generational ties appear to be more indigenous, the markers of the charro cowboy community can be read from the very words that they use to describe certain items. Due to the charro cowboy community's rural ties, certain Spanish words are cut shorter and are harder to understand for someone who did not grow up listening to this particular type of accent. Vicente often asks his charro cowboy peers to repeat words further evidencing the fact that he is not a native with a legitimate claim of the charro cowboy tradition. The charro cowboy vocabulary is just another form of identifying legitimacy within the community.

Alejandro is an 18-year-old rookie charro cowboy with no generational ties. He also participates in *charreadas* with a team and has become a top competitor in the *jineto de toro*. Unlike Vicente and Mere, Alejandro has no recent indigenous ties but also does not have the charro cowboy tradition identifiers. Although he is below five foot five inches tall, he has blue eyes, bright blonde hair, and a lighter complexion. Alejandro comes from a middle class family and his parents graduated high school. His interest in the charro cowboy community started back in elementary school when he saw a charro cowboy on his horse during Mexico's National Charro Day. He grew up in a town outside of Guadalajara, Mexico where charro cowboy teams are the most common. Since his parents have a disposable income, they were able to enroll Alejandro into a charro cowboy school. Charro cowboy schools are operated by charro cowboy *jefes* trying to make money from wealthier potential charro cowboy rookies and are often linked to the charro team that they manage. These schools are often promoted by the Mexican Federation of

Charros because of their continued goal to make the charro cowboy tradition more mainstream in Mexican society. These schools often have to pay a fee to the Mexican Federation of Charros in order to be deemed legitimate.

Alejandro is a graduate of his charro cowboy *jefe*'s school and was placed into the team after his graduation from the program due to his promising talent. His charro cowboy *jefe* saw great potential and promise and Alejandro was his top student. In contrast to Vicente and Mere, Alejandro reported no incidents of discrimination for being a charro cowboy rookie but rather moments of embarrassment. This is probably because Alejandro blends with other charro cowboys with generational ties since they also tend to be lighter of complexion, colored eyes, or lighter hair shades. His embarrassing moments are centered largely on incidents where he lacked the knowledge to "pass" as a generational charro cowboy. Alejandro "passes" as a generational charro cowboy until he starts talking because he lacks the knowledge that is usually learned in childhood socialization among generational charro cowboys. In my observations of Alejandro, many charro cowboys with generational ties, both from the older and younger generation, did not refer to Alejandro as "garbage" in the way that they did to Vicente and Mere. Comments about his charro cowboy rookie status only revealed itself when Alejandro interacted with other generational charro cowboys.

In particular, on one occasion when I was watching Alejandro compete, a group of older and experiences of charro cowboys were drinking on the sidelines near the curve of the *lienzo*. One of the older charro cowboys was on Alejandro's team while the other charro cowboys were from the opposing teams. The bull that Alejandro was riding during this particular competition was angry and massive. Many spectators made comments about how dangerous it would be to ride this bull since the previous charro cowboy contender had been wounded and rushed to hospital. Since Alejandro was significantly smaller in statue, many spectators anxiously waited to witness how Alejandro would handle himself with this dangerous bull. The charro cowboy with no affiliation to Alejandro took a shot of tequila as he commented on Alejandro's bravery and management of the massive beast. The older charro cowboy on Alejandro team poured himself a shot as he stated, "And you wouldn't even know that he is new." The others looked at Alejandro more closely and commented collectively, "I guess you're right." These same men had been previously commenting on other charro cowboy rookies in a more critical and harsh manner. Yet, their view of Alejandro did not correspond with their views of charro cowboy rookies therefore they were less harsh. This did not mean that they disregarded their beliefs about generational charro cowboys, however, Alejandro fitted more closely with the charro cowboy canons of taste. Charro cowboys with generational ties still believed that generational ties to the community are the only way for an authentic charro cowboy identity.

On another occasion, Alejandro mentioned that he often finds himself trying to copy what other charro cowboys are doing in order to not be read as a charro cowboy rookie. This is not rare since many charro cowboy rookies often commented on trying to emulate the very charro cowboys they admired. Since he went to a charro cowboy school, he was able to learn the proper charro cowboy terms about the tradition. He stated that a whole week was dedicated to the proper vocabulary and general etiquette of the charro cowboy tradition. However, he was not able to learn about mannerism and styles of greeting that are unique to the charro cowboy community because these mannerisms and styles occur more organically in conversation.

For example, during one of my observations of Alejandro, I witness him interact with other charro cowboys during a particularly important *charreada*. Alejandro was talking to two other charro cowboys from his team. Both of these charro cowboys were young and had generational ties. In the midst their conversation, an older charro cowboy walked his horse by the charro cowboys. He raised his hand slightly above his head with his drink and slightly nodded at the charro cowboys. While the other two charro cowboys without a single hesitation lifted their cups to the charro cowboy, Alejandro stumbled. He looked nervous and barely made eye contact with the older charro cowboy. Later as he were talking about the events of that day, I asked Alejandro why he had looked so nervous in front of the older charro cowboy. He stated:

> I do not know... (laughs). I still feel strange around older charro cowboys because you never know what they will say to you. They are not shy to tell you what they really think. And to tell you the truth... (laughs) I never know when I should lift my cup to someone.
>
> (Interview, 2014)

Alejandro often finds himself flustered even though he can pass as a generational charro cowboy because he knows that he does not have the identifiers of a generational charro cowboy.

Whether a newcomer knows the proper mannerisms and styles of the charro cowboy tradition is not what is in question. What is in question is the element of legitimacy and authenticity that seems to automatically disqualify someone from the label of charro cowboy. These mannerisms and styles become tools to demonstrate membership and honorific distinction. Veblen argued:

> These accomplishments may, in some sense, be classed as branches of learning. Beside and beyond these there is a further range of social facts which shade off from the region of learning into that of physical habit and dexterity. Such are what is known as manners and breeding, polite usage, decorum, and formal and ceremonial observances generally. This class of facts are even more immediately and obtrusively presented to the observation, and they therefore more widely and more imperatively insisted on as required evidences of a reputable degree of leisure. It is

worth while to remark that all that class of ceremonial observances which are classed under the general head of manners hold a more important place in the esteem of men during the stage of culture at which conspicuous leisure has the greatest vogue as a mark of reputability, than at later stages of the cultural development.

(Veblen 1899, 22–23)

This barbaric habit of distinction indicates that the well-bred gentleman yields more honor and prestige than those who do not follow such social mores. The charro cowboy community holds similar branches of learning that serve as evidence of a reputable degree of charro cowboy identity. A great deal of time is spent on teaching young charro cowboys the mannerisms and styles of the tradition that serve as symbolic forms of dominance and mastery. Outsiders and newcomers will be unable to submerge themselves into the charro cowboy community without being easily identified by their lack of "good breeding".

Charro cowboy rookies like Vicente, Mere, and Alejandro are examples of the discrimination faced in the charro cowboy community as well as in larger Mexican community. Mexico is not immune to discrimination based on skin color, gender, class, and sexual orientation. These facts contradict the charro cowboy belief that the community has conquered these problems or achieved utopia. Due to the charro cowboy tradition's connection to Spanish colonization, the caste system placed on Mexico colonial society had lasting consequences for many indigenous communities and often leads to their continuous marginalization. Mexican racism differs from the United States in the sense that much of the racial marginalization is based on an indigenous past and its connection to class (Schaefer 2008). Further, discrimination based on race, class, gender, and sexual orientation is further dramatized by regional and cultural descent (Nutini and Isaac 2009). Since the charro cowboy community is a subset of Mexican culture, the discrimination that has been documented here has been based on the consequence of political power and struggle since the Spanish colonial period. Vicente and Mere are from Mexico State that is often categorized as having more poor and indigenous urban people. The people of the Mexico City categorize charro cowboys from other regions in Mexico as being cheap or lacking culture.

Alejandro's home state of Jalisco is one of the originating states of the charro cowboy tradition. As I traveled to competitions in the state of Jalisco, I saw various signs that celebrated elements of white supremacy, with signs on town entrances' that read, "proudly white". While Alejandro's visual identity can be read as a charro cowboy, his home state further carries prestige in the community. Once again, Alejandro has a slight advantage since he is of a higher socio-economic class than Vicente and Mere who were born on the outskirts of Mexico City. This is only until he enters into social interactions with generational charro cowboys because of his lack of ease and charro cowboy terminology. Alejandro, Vicente, and Mere all have to learn about the tradition based on what other charro cowboy are doing around them. Because charro cowboy rookies tend to socialize among themselves, their behavior during *charreadas* is even more noticeable.

Charro cowboy rookies emulate charro cowboys that they think have prestige and honor. In the case of Vicente, he looks up to his charro cowboy *jefe* who could be classified as a being part of the charro cowboy leisure class. While there are charro cowboy rookies that want to participate in the community for the genuine desire to become a charro cowboy and learn the tradition, some charro cowboy rookies are more motivated by for the prestige and honor they hope to achieve by participating. Anderson's (1978) research on black urban poor and working class people analyses the mechanism in which people with low socioeconomic status negotiate their own measure of self-worth and social standards. This resonates with Veblen's (1899) arguments about vicarious consumption because the ways in which lower ranking men in predominately predatory society try to appear more honorable. Veblen stated, "The need of vicarious leisure, or conspicuous consumption of service, is a dominant incentive to the keeping of servants" (Veblen 1899, 30). In the case of the charro cowboy rookies, the notion of possible prestige and honor fuels their motivation to continue to participate even though charro cowboy rookies face different forms of discriminations.

Charro cowboy rookies of low socio-economic status use the community to enhance their self-worth. This is because the charro cowboy community is still seen as a symbol of Mexican nationalism and its contemporary imagery in Mexico radiates honor and prestige. Charro cowboy rookies with indigenous ties are often discriminated against to the point that they choose to leave the charro cowboy community for the American rodeo; however, this is often short lived because American rodeo is seen as less prestigious and poor value to the charro cowboy community. The charro cowboy community views the American rodeo as a lower ranking form of equestrian skill because many charro cowboys believe that the American rodeo eliminates traditions such as the charro cowboy form of dress, the charro cowboy saddle, the commemoration of the past, etc. The American rodeo has similar elements to the charro cowboy community such as aspects of horse reining and bull riding, however there is no prerequisite to participate in American rodeo other than being willing to take the risk. The American rodeo is also deemed to be less exclusive than the charro cowboy tradition, therefore lowering its value to many charro cowboys. While there is some investment of money when wanting to participate in the American rodeo, it does not compare to the hefty economic costs of participating in the charro cowboy community. Many charro cowboy rookies may look at the American rodeo as a way to escape continuous discrimination or as a way of participating in a sport with lower costs; however, the cost-effectiveness of the American rodeo does not provide enough incentive to permanently leave the charro cowboy community since there are no socially honorific or prestigious rewards.

César, a once aspiring charro cowboy, stopped competing with the charro cowboy tradition because he never felt accepted or appreciated. César, a talented 25-year-old at the time, loved bull riding and had qualified for national competitions. He left the charro cowboy community for the American rodeo because he felt that the community was full of pretentious people who looked down on people who were of a darker complexion. "They did not allow me to grow. You can only take so much abuse." In 2015, César was competing in the United States as a bull rider and was happy. He missed competing in *charreadas* because he described the American rodeo as being less connected to tradition and customs. However, he explained that he had bills to pay now that he was planning on getting married. He stated that he is often jealous of his charro cowboy rookie friends that are still competing in Mexico. While leaving the charro cowboy community might be identified as a form of resistance against the discrimination that charro cowboy rookies experience, the American rodeo does not provide the same type of prestige and honor that the participating in the charro cowboy community does. Ultimately, some charro cowboy rookies would rather endure forms of discrimination from their charro cowboy peers than belong at the American rodeo community that is labeled "rodeo clowns" by the charro cowboy community.

The socialization of charro cowboy rookies with indigenous ties, charro cowboy rookies with no indigenous ties, and generational charro cowboys is essential to a sense of belonging in the community. While generational charro cowboys are socialized at birth, differences surface when examining socio-economic status. Lower income generational charro cowboys accentuate their charro cowboy legacy and denounce those who use money to gain access to the community. Charro cowboy rookies face some discrimination based upon class and ethnicity. Generational charro cowboys are very protective the charro cowboy tradition and may engage in forms of discrimination to center legitimacy upon "bloodlines" and charro cowboy legacy. However, charro cowboy rookies from higher socio-economic classes and no indigenous ties can "pass" as generational charro cowboys until their lack of cultural capital and childhood socialization raises questions about their identity and legitimacy. Even though some charro cowboy rookies experience resistance from their charro cowboy peers, they would rather endure the discrimination than be permanently labeled as a "rodeo clown". The charro cowboy community provides them with the prestige, honor, and sense of nationalism to make them want to continue to participate in competitions even if they do not make much money.

## Notes

1 A reality series called *Los Cowboys* (2015) depicted the lives of a wealthy charro cowboy family in Los Angeles, California. These individuals are recognized in the charro cowboy community in the southwest of the United States, however, their goal remains centered on gaining notoriety among the various important associations of Mexico. Their main goal, like other charro cowboy teams, is to qualify for the national championships hosted in Guadalajara, Jalisco and Pachuca, Hidalgo Mexico.

2 Torbio's apology was due the fact that his yell was very loud and powerful causing
me to flinch like Jorge. While his son was the direct target of his sanctions, his yell
had a powerful effect those who were around him. He apologized for scaring me
because I was his guest.

## References

Anderson, Elijah. *A Place on the Corner.* Chicago: University of Chicago Press. 1978.

Baudrillard, Jean. *America.* New York: Verso. 1989.

Brandth, Berit and Marit S. Haugen. "Doing Rural Masculinity: From Logging to
Outfield Tourism." *Journal of Gender Studies,* vol. 14 (2005): 13–22.

Butler, Judith. *Gender Trouble: Feminism and the Subversion of Identity.* New York:
Routledge. 1990.

Connell, R. W., and J. W. Messerschmidt. "Hegemonic Masculinity: Rethinking the
Concept." *Gender and Society,* vol. 19 (2005): 829–859.

Kimmel, Michael. *Manhood in America: A Cultural History.* New York: The Free
Press. 1997.

Kimmel, Michael. *Manhood in America: A Cultural History Guyland: The Perilous
World Where Boys Become Men.* New York, NY: Harper Collins Publishers. 2008.

Moore, Valerie A. "The Collaborative Emergence of Race in Children's Play: A Case
Study of Two Summer Camps." *Social Problems,* vol. 49 (2002): 58–78.

Moss, Kirby. *The Color of Class: Poor Whites and the Paradox of Privilege.* Philadel-
phia, Pennsylvania: University of Pennsylvania Press. 2010.

Nutini, Hugo and Barry Isaac. *Social Stratification in Central Mexico 1500–2000.*
Austin, Texas: University of Texas Press. 2009.

Riesman, David. *The Lonely Crowd: A Study of the Changing American Character.*
New Haven, Connecticut: Yale University Press. 1961.

Sands, Kathleen M. *Charrería Mexicana: An Equestrian Folk Tradition.* Tucson: University of Arizona Press, 1993.

Schaefer, Richard T. ed. *Encyclopedia of Race, Ethnicity and Society.* Thousand Oaks,
California: Sage. 2008.

West, Candace and Don H. Zimmerman. "Doing Gender." *Gender and Society,* vol. 1
(1987): 125–151.

Veblen, Thorstein. *The Theory of the Leisure Class: An Economic Study of Institutions.*
New York: Reprint by The New American Library. 1953[1899].

# 4 The ranking of charro cowboy women

Some of the charro cowboys from yesterday are still drinking this early afternoon. A small group of children, wearing sombreros and boots, sit next their mothers as they watch the lienzo [arena]. There is a small market outside selling hats, cowboy boots, sombreros, vests, and even specialized handmade blankets. The music is blaring from the surrounding speakers and taco stands work on cooking meat and preparing alcoholic drinks for the people standing in their lands. A group of young girls walk in into the lienzo and head toward the stands. They are wearing tight blue jeans, tank tops, bright make-up. One woman has long brown hair that is braided to the side of her hair. They are stopped by a group of charro cowboys who invite them to their drinking spot. They girls happily follow. A group of charro cowboy wives stare disapprovingly as the girls take their first shot with the group of charro cowboy men.

(Observation, July 2015)

Charro cowboy rookies with no generational ties and lower class charro cowboys with generational ties are not the only ones who face continuous marginalization in the community. Women have a space in the charro cowboy community; however, it is separate and not equal to charro cowboy men. Although I have argued that the charro cowboy tradition has what Veblen would identify as, peaceable traits, the patriarchal social structure associated with barbaric and predatory habits rank women and objectionable men as secondary. Most women recognize and accept their secondary role due to their early socialization into the charro cowboy community, although a small number of women express interest in changing these dynamics. Despite the secondary role of women, some charro cowboy women reinforce and suppress the voices of women who do wish to invoke change and the restructuring of these power dynamics. Even though their place in the community is one of subservience, charro cowboy women who have been socialized into the community hardly ever resist their position. Women who do resist are often faced by harsh reinforcement of other charro cowboy women and men to conform to the charro cowboy traditions.

In the charro cowboy community, women are categorized in one of the three following: 1) charro cowboy female family members (i.e. charro cowboy wives or daughters), 2) charro cowboy love interests, 3) *otra* or other (i.e. a female outsider). Each category yields a different level of respect and courtesy from charro cowboy men. Charro cowboy female family members are ranked at the top of the hierarchy and are approached with respect These charro cowboy women have power, not over charro cowboy men specifically, but over other women below them in the hierarchy. Charro cowboy female family members are protected from charro cowboys who have questionable romantic intentions by members of the community. Since charro cowboy men have more agency with regards to how they treat women, they are rarely reprimanded for being disrespectful or sexual harassing women they deem to be low status.

It is evident that the role of women in the charro cowboy tradition is secondary to that of men. I have affirmed previously that in barbaric and predatory culture, exploitation and visible success are designated as honorable. Therefore, it would not be incorrect to assume that these aspects of barbaric and predatory culture are applied to how men and women interact in the charro cowboy community. In the charro cowboy community, women recognize their secondary status to men since they are aware that their role in the *charreada* is an aesthetic one rather than a competitive one. Veblen stated, "In such a predatory group of hunters it comes to be the able-bodied men's office to fight and hunt. The women do what other work there is to do—other members who are unfit for man's work being for this purpose classed with the women" (Veblen 1899, 7). Charro cowboy wives, daughters, and love interests often find themselves in a subservient position due to the patriarchal division of labor that labels their work as trivial.[1] Although these women perform meaningful domestic labor, the influence of the predatory and barbaric culture marginalizes their work when juxtaposed with charro cowboy men's labor.

The charro cowboy identity is also heavily dependent on the romantic interests of other women because there is value in being wanted by women. Courting practices in the charro cowboy community are not unique , nevertheless, women serve an important function to elevate the status of men. The manner in which charro cowboy men behave towards women is indicative of what Veblen identified as the barbarian status of women in a culture dominated by predatory and barbaric habits. Men, according to Veblen, in the predatory phase of life, praise aggression. Evidence of prowess is not only encouraged by charro cowboy men, but are also necessary to demonstrate success and the acquisition of women is no exception. Veblen stated, "Likewise the earliest form of ownership is an ownership of women by the able-bodied men of the community" (Veblen 1899, 12). Just as younger charro cowboy view *charreadas* in terms of trophies to be won, the same association can be applied to the women they desire. While there are some charro cowboys that reject the "womanizing charro cowboy", there are some who proudly identify with it.

In this chapter, I will argue that the role of women is reinforced and reproduced throughout generations. The hierarchy of women in the charro cowboy community also plays a role in how women are "respected" and approached by charro cowboy men. Further, I will explore the socialization of women in to the charro cowboy community with generational ties compared to non-generational ties. I will note the important differences and illustrate how those who resist charro cowboy culture are maneuvered back into submission. I will document how charro cowboy men approach various rankings of charro cowboy women as love interests. Lastly, I examine the role of charro cowboy women as *escaramuzas* in charro cowboy competitions (*charreadas*) and how they view themselves and how charro cowboy men view them. I argue that women who compete as *escaramuzas* tend to have a high income, generational ties, and are seen as respectable members of the community compared to other women. Yet, their participation and competition is secondary to charro cowboy men.

## The highest degree of female respectability

The patriarchal structure of the charro cowboy community positions charro cowboy men above women; however, within that patriarchal structure, women in the community are not all treated equally by charro cowboy men. Charro cowboy female family members have the highest acclamation of charro cowboy men and other women in the community. This is because they have a direct social tie to charro cowboy men as their wives, daughters, aunts, grandmothers, etc. Many of them even have generational ties to the community. Although the charro cowboy community is a highly patriarchal structure, the household or the domestic sphere is still recognized by charro cowboy men as the place where women dominate and set the rules. Further, charro cowboy female family members are often protected by charro cowboy men from potentially disrespectful men who wish to romance them without the promise of commitment. If these important women are disrespected, charro cowboy men may feel pressure to defend the honor of their women, thus re-establishing order through violence. These charro cowboy women acknowledge that they have some authority over women who are below them, but serve as tools for charro cowboy men's identity and honor.

Charro cowboy men, in particular the older generation of charro cowboy, spend most of their downtime in competitions drinking, and smoking cigars with their team members. Their charro cowboy female members are expected to be present at every competition and cheer them on as they compete. Many charro cowboys start drinking alcohol at 10:00AM, from when the competition begins to after midnight when the competition is over. As stated earlier, Veblen argued that drinking alcohol or consuming mind altering drugs can be framed as honorific for men in a barbaric and predatory culture. Women, however, are not included in these behaviors. Veblen states:

> Infirmities induced by over-indulgence are among some peoples freely recognized as manly attributes...The same invidious distinction adds force to the current disapproval of any indulgence of this kind of the part of women, minors, and inferiors. This invidious traditional distinction has

not lost its force even among the more advanced peoples of today. Where the example set by the leisure class retains its imperative force in the regulation of the conventionalities, it is observable that the women still in great measure practice the same traditional continence with regard to stimulants.

(Veblen 1899, 34)

Women, especially female family members, during competitions are not supposed to consume alcohol or get drunk in public. This does not mean that it never happens, however, women must be extra cautious because this type of behavior is seen as low class and disrespectful to their husbands. Although most charro cowboy men will leave the competition drunk, female family members are expected to be sober. Even though it is socially unacceptable for women to drink alcohol, they do keep the extra bottles of tequila in their purses for their husbands.

During competitions and practice sessions, female family members sit together and keep each other company. Since competitions can last all day, they mostly sit and talk to one another about different aspects of their lives. Charro cowboy female family members are easy to spot because they are usually the best dressed women in these spaces. They are beautiful women with perfected makeup, styled hair, expensive cowboy boots, and fancy and expensive purses. Charro cowboy female family members with generational ties, like their male counterparts, hold the same views about the authentic and legitimate charro cowboy identity in regards to bloodlines. They were often more vocal about bloodlines as being the only true element of charro cowboy authenticity and legitimacy. Many charro cowboy female family members argued that they could spot a "fake charro cowboy" from a kilometer away. Linda, a 52-year-old charro cowboy family member argued that newcomers lack the character and family necessary to be great charro cowboys. Linda referenced her four decades of observations to support her argument by saying that the charro cowboy community should exclude charro cowboy rookies that do not fit the image and character of the community.

Generational charro cowboy women are more comfortable in charro cowboy spaces and culture because they have been socialized into its customs since birth. These women present confidence that is not found in charro cowboy love interests without generational ties and female outsiders. For example, Yessica, a 32-year-old mother of two with generational ties, described that she is the most comfortable around other charro cowboy families. She stated:

The charreadas are like family gatherings. My family is a real charro cowboy family and have been to lots of charreadas throughout my life. My job is to cheer for our charro cowboys and I have fun with the other women. Some people may find it boring, but I love it!

(Interview, 2015)

Yessica's sentiments are shared by many other generational women who do not question their position in the community. She sees herself as valuable because she plays a role in how charro cowboy culture and tradition is reproduced and is surrounded by other women and men who believe in the significance of the charro cowboy tradition.

In an earlier chapter, I discussed charro cowboy socialization and the role of the charro cowboy father. While often socialization can become violent between father and son, charro cowboy female family members do not necessarily prevent this violence. Charro cowboy wives, in particular charro cowboy women with generational ties, encourage their sons to listen to their fathers and also expect their sons to become charro cowboys themselves. They apply almost the same pressure on their male offspring as their husband because charro cowboy female family members also want to continue, reproduce, and enact the charro cowboy traditions so that they survive future generations. Charro cowboy wives and grandmothers with generational ties believe that "real" men are created in the *lienzo* or the competition arena. Like their male counterparts, the charro cowboy tradition is in their bloodlines and they tend to be highly critical of charro cowboy rookies. They tend to express openly racist and discriminatory remarks toward charro cowboy rookies, regardless of age.

Unmarried and young charro cowboy daughters are expected to become charro cowboy women with a dignified and respectable status, therefore, these women are the most protected and hold the most value in the community. Charro cowboy men and older charro cowboy female family members spend a lot of time teaching young charro cowboy girls about the gendered rules of respectability. While young male charro cowboy adolescents can enjoy being around the company of older charro cowboys, charro cowboy girls are taught to never approach a group of charro cowboy men unless they are invited by their parents. For example, Esmeralda, an 18-year-old with generational ties, stated that if she wanted to ask her father for something, she had to wait until each member of the group had finished their conversation. This could potentially take a long time; therefore, most young women ask ranch hands to handle their requests. By having a lower ranking male carry out their request, these women can avoid potentially uncomfortable situations. Esmeralda also explained that she had been taught by her mother and aunts to never drink with a group of men by herself, to always look presentable in public (i.e. wear makeup and modest clothing), and to never openly argue with a charro cowboy man.

Esmeralda has been to *charreadas* since she was an infant and has made many friends with other charro cowboy daughters and sons. Like Yessica, she views *charreadas* as a family gathering and is often very excited to attend these events; however, she did speak of annoyance when it comes to the overtly masculine characteristics of the charro cowboy community. She explained:

> I cannot do anything without them watching me. I always have to have my brother [Esmeralda's brother is 12] with me if I want to go do anything. It was okay when I was 14… laughs…but not at my age. I have trained him to not tell my parents everything I do… but as he gets older … laughs… the same ten pesos are not enough to shut him up!

Betty: What kind of things are you referring to?

Esmeralda: When I drink or smoke a cigarette. He is nosy but money works for now.

Esmeralda explains that her independence is limited in the community because she feels that she is constantly watched by charro cowboys. She mentioned in our conversations cases where her father's friends told her father she was talking to an unknown charro cowboy rookie. By having her younger brother, Enrique, follow her around her parents feel that they can protect Esmeralda's respectability within the charro cowboy community. She bribes her brother in order to be able to smoke a cigarette or take a shot of tequila with her other friends because her brother is often asked by her mother to report on Esmeralda's behavior. Even though I have only known Esmeralda and her family for a few years, I was also expected to report on her behavior because I was considered an older charro cowboy female family member. Esmeralda is denied the agency to drink and smoke cigarettes without the watchful eye of a chaperone, even though she is of legal age. This mechanism of protection is not unique to the charro cowboy community, nevertheless is reveals the significant lengths that charro cowboy men and women will go to protect the respectability of a lady.

Charro cowboy female respectability can be tied into patriarchal notions of virginity and virtue before the sexual revolution. This notion of respectability is further connected to social relations of Mexican colonialism. According to Patricia Seed (1988), a historian of Latin American culture, marriage promises in colonial Mexico were highly respected and cultural values were encoded into a system of honor. Seed stated in her work, "Marriage Promises and the Value of a Woman's Testimony in Colonial Mexico":

Honor stemmed from either superior birth or moral integrity. During the sixteenth and seventeenth centuries in Spain as well as in Spain's colonies, honor primarily signified moral integrity. For women in colonial Mexico, this dimension of honor meant premarital chastity and postmarital fidelity; for men, it meant courage and fidelity to promises made. Although the criteria for honorable conduct were different for men and women, the behavior of one sex could influence the honor of the other. Since a woman's status was defined by her relationship to men, the prestige of her father, brother, or husband established her standing in the community; a lapse in courage by her male kin disgraced her as well as them. Yet a woman's sexual activity and thus honor similarly could affect the status of her male relatives.

(Seed 1988)

Spanish colonial dimensions of honor and female respectability resonate with the charro cowboy tradition's notion of femininity and respectability because its tradition stems from Spanish colonialism. Mexico is still a highly Catholic and socially conservative country and it is not surprising to learn that the charro cowboy community's ideas of virtue and respectability in the context of women is rooted in religious conservatism.

Seed's (1988) understanding of colonial Mexico's courtship practices can also be extended to Veblen's framing of the status of women in a dominant predatory and barbaric society. As I have argued, women are categorized by high ranking men with honorable status as being less worthy of the respect attributed to their male counterparts. Women are used as a tool to show prowess of masculine identity, further demonstrating that charro cowboy men are evaluated by their peers in terms of their honor and desirability. Charro cowboy women's relations to charro cowboy men is veiled with elements of ownership and conquest, an important feature of Veblen's understanding of marriage. Veblen stated:

> After the habit of appropriated captured women has hardened into custom, and so given rise on the one hand to a form of marriage resting on coercion, and on the other hand to a concept of ownership, a development of certain secondary features of the institution so inaugurated is to be looked for. In time this coercive ownership—marriage receives the sanction of the popular taste and morality. It comes to rest in men's habits of thought as the right form of marriage relation, and it comes at the same time to be gratifying to men's sense of beauty and honor. The growing predilection for mastery and coercion, as a manly trait, together with the growing moral and aesthetic approbation of marriage on a basis of coercion and ownership, will affect the tastes of the men most immediately and most strongly; but since the men are the superior class, whose views determine the current views of the community, their common sense in the matter will shape the current canons of taste in its own image.
>
> (Veblen 1899, 507)

Here Veblen highlights the formation of marriage as it is shaped by mastery and coercion. This framing does not negate the decision of charro cowboy women to choose their suitor, nevertheless, this important argument allows us to understand why charro cowboy women are pressured to view marriage as the ultimate accomplishment in their lives. Charro cowboy men shape the current cannons of taste that separate women as worthy of marriage proposals and those who serve as sexual amusement.

Due to the highly patriarchal nature of the charro cowboy community, many charro cowboy men take it upon themselves to preserve the virtue of their female family members. Charro cowboy female family members are dependent on their relationship with their charro cowboy men because their respectability and honor is dependent on the respect bestowed by them. Charro cowboy female family members who disgrace themselves by denying notions of female respectability and honor (i.e. engaging in premarital sex) not only disgrace themselves, but also disgrace their family's reputation. Therefore, having male chaperones to observe the behavior of young charro cowboy women is not uncommon because it protects both the charro cowboy female family member and the charro cowboy men in her life. The protection is greater for her father than her own reputation.

Esmeralda understands that her actions, smoking cigarettes and drinking with her friends, could be perceived as deviant and inappropriate by other members of her community. Her brother, although young, has a responsibility to his family to report misconduct because he also has a duty to protect his older sister's virtue and respectability. Although Esmeralda is only smoking cigarettes and occasionally drinking tequila, this is only acceptable for charro cowboy men and their enactment of rural masculine identity. She is breaking a gendered rule of agency. While women in the charro cowboy community do drink and smoke cigarettes, charro cowboy female family members are not expected to participate in such behavior publically or discuss it in within the earshot of their husbands and boyfriends.

This once again can be framed within the understanding of the "barbarian status of women" in predatory and barbaric culture. It is evident when Veblen stated:

> The accepted scheme of life or consensus of opinions which guides the conduct of men in such a predatory group and decides what may properly be done, of course comprise a great variety of details; but it is, after all, a single scheme—a more or less organic whole—a somewhat consistent and characteristic body of culture... Whatever may be the immediate point or object of his thinking, the frame of mind which governs his aim and manner of reasoning in passing on any given point of conduct is, on the whole, the habitual frame of mind which experience and have enforced upon him. Individuals whose sense of what is right and good departs widely from the accepted views suffer some repression and in case of an extreme divergence they are eliminated from the effective life of the group through ostracism.
>
> (Veblen 1899, 506–507)

Ostracism in a powerful tool of repression for charro cowboy women who want to depart from the accepted norms. Charro cowboy women who refuse to conform to the highly patriarchal expectations of women are subject to possibly permanent exclusion. Unlike charro cowboy young men who have the freedom to experiment with drinking and tobacco, these young women, as we will see in the example below, are more accountable for their actions because their image is connected with their father's family name.

For example, charro cowboy women, especially daughters, are expected to refrain from premarital sex. A charro cowboy female family member with a questionable sexual past is likely to be highly marginalized by members of their community and may face being officially excluded from the charro cowboy community; however, permanent exclusion is rare if charro cowboy female family members marry a charro cowboy man. Ana Cristina, a 25-year-old from a generational charro cowboy family, found herself in a vulnerable position when she was a teenager. Ana Cristiana was born and raised in rural Jalisco with five of her siblings (two sisters and three brothers). Like many other generational charro cowboy female members, she grew up in the community and attended many *charreadas* throughout her life. When Ana Cristiana was 16, she met Jacobo, ten years her senior, while attending a *charreada* in Mexico City. Jacobo was engaged to another woman at the time; yet, he carried on a romantic relationship with Ana Cristiana regardless. At first, Ana Cristiana kept their relationship a secret from her family since she did not want her father to intervene in her relationship. She recognized that she would be vulnerable to punishment if her relationship was made public. Ana Cristiana stated:

> I was in love but very stupid (laughs). I was young and did not care what happened to me as long as I had Jacobo in my life. But… my uncle's friend told my father and I was kicked out my house. My mother did not talk to me for a month. I stayed at my friend's house in town.
> Betty: What did your uncle's friend tell your father?
> Ana Cristina: Well… that I was acting like a whore in Mexico City. (long pause) He told him that Jacobo had a fiancé and that I knew. (soft sniffle) And that I didn't care.

Ana Cristiana and Jacobo's relationship ended as soon as her family was notified. Their relationship was discovered after Ana Cristina was seen leaving Jacobo's hotel room in the early morning. Although Ana Cristiana was 16 at the time and Jacobo was significantly older, her parents granted more importance to loss of respectability and virtue than the fact that Ana Cristina was taken advantage of by an older man. Ana Cristiana referenced love and rebellion as the source of her family troubles.

Ana Cristiana was able to reinstate her reputation by apologizing to her family and more specifically, apologizing to her father for bringing this scandal upon her family name. Her actions not only tarnished her own reputation, but also her father's in the charro cowboy community. This reflects how Ana Cristiana's relationship with her family was based on the ownership of her father. Her actions were not her own, but rather her father's to control. Jacobo was never confronted for his actions since Ana Cristiana was held responsible by her family for engaging in the relationship in the first place. Men in the charro cowboy community are characterized as not having control over their sexual desires and therefore women must bear the burden of making sure they are respected.

Now at 25, Ana Cristiana is the mother of two small children and has her own charro cowboy husband. The passing of time played a significant role in healing her own reputation as well as her family's. Further, Ana Cristina stated that her family has never discussed the incident since she apologized and was able to return home. Although it was a significantly emotional situation, Ana Cristiana said "Yo como si nada (It is like as if nothing had happened)" when around other members of the charro cowboy community. This, however, does not necessarily mean that people have forgotten about Ana Cristiana's past behavior, but other people simply no longer mention it to her or her family. Since she is married with children, Ana Cristiana is granted the respect and dignity that charro cowboy female family members receive in the community. Due to her past, Ana Cristiana must work hard to retain her reputation, even though she was only 16 when her reputation was tarnished.

Due to the negative consequences of having a questionable reputation or past, many charro cowboy female family members will attempt to hide any perceived deviant behavior from their charro cowboy families. Ana Cristiana is not the first charro cowboy daughter to be romanced by an older charro cowboy or to have sex before marriage. Any indiscretions between charro cowboy female family members are usually kept secret or ignored by the community. Charro cowboy women like Esmeralda have to hide their drinking and smoking from their families in order to avoid situations where their reputation would be deemed questionable. In the case of Cielo, a 27-year-old with generational ties, she has to hide the majority of her private life from her parents. Her father is an older charro cowboy with a respectable legacy and her mother is the daughter of a wealthy family. Cielo is one of five siblings who all participate in the charro cowboy tradition in some manner. She lives with her family and their house is located about 20 minutes outside a conservative small town in Jalisco named after a patron saint. Cielo did not finish high school (although that is not uncommon for this area) but she owns several cows that she uses to generate an income. In the charro cowboy community, Cielo is recognized as a hardworking woman from a respectable charro cowboy family.

From an outside perspective, Cielo's life is very common of a single charro cowboy daughter because she still lives with her parents while helping around the ranch; however, Cielo is a lesbian and is not out to her family. Her family, like many members of the charro cowboy community are religious and socially conservative and have negative points of view about homosexuality. They view homosexuality as a disease and rarely attribute homosexuality to women since sexuality is supposed to be suppressed by all women. Cielo acknowledges that coming out to her family would have a negative impact on, not only her, but also her whole family because they would never accept it. Cielo never stated clearly that there would be physical violence but it was implied. Therefore, she is very secretive about her personal life and tries to not "show" her queerness to other members of the charro cowboy community. Cielo only trusted me with this secret after becoming aware that I was also gay. Cielo's lesbianism contradicts charro cowboy notions of female respectability since charro cowboy female members are considered to be crucial in charro cowboy identity and characterization. Women, in the charro cowboy tradition, can be framed as being trophies of charro cowboy men.

While all women of different categories can be trophies, charro cowboy female members are the ultimate trophies with the highest value. Veblen explains, "The man's prowess was still primarily the group's prowess, and the possessor of the booty felt himself to be primarily the keeper of the honour of his group." A charro cowboy female member who is a lesbian may be perceived as a threat to charro cowboy masculinity and authority.

Cielo makes sure she never reveals any elements of her queerness by refraining from being seen in public spaces with other queer people. For example, Cielo's upbringing reflects many of the experiences witnessed in this study. She was taught by her mother to always look presentable in public and at *charreadas* and to avoid drinking and smoking in public. Therefore, Cielo wears makeup and dresses up like her straight friends in order to blend into spaces predominantly occupied by members of the charro cowboy community. Cielo's closest friends are not in the charro cowboy community and she believes in keeping the two domains separate from each other. Cielo explains:

> It is better this way. Being less obvious. My friends do not understand why I care [about the charro cowboy tradition] My parents cannot deal with it.
> Betty: What would happen?
> Cielo: My mother would go to church…(laughs). She is really good friends with the priest but she would not tell anyone else. It would be too embarrassing for her. She … She would not like other people asking her about it. My father would… I am not sure if he would…he would ever recognize it. My siblings are like my parents. Better to keep it a secret between us (laughs).
>
> (Interview, 2014)

Being honest about her sexual orientation for Cielo may lead her to risk the acceptance of her charro cowboy family. Although Cielo articulated that she might be happier not being in the charro cowboy community, she would never be able to escape where she comes from because the charro cowboy tradition is in her blood. The significance of tradition is greater than the comforts of escape and freedom to be herself. She recognizes that the charro cowboy community may label her as not respectable thereby damaging her reputation as a hardworking charro cowboy. Cielo also expressed continuous feelings of stress and anxiety that she feels due to constantly having to hide her life from members of her family and the community. Although Cielo is not unique in this case, her story illustrates the great lengths that charro cowboy women of generational ties go to in order to adhere to the standards of respectability of the charro cowboy community.

Cielo's anxieties regarding the revelation of her sexual orientation demonstrate how powerful the canons of taste are in the charro cowboy community. Her lesbianism placed her ambiguously in relation to the ownership of men because an openly gay woman would not be manipulated and coerced through the charro cowboy courtship process. Cielo recognizes the real and potentially violent consequences of living in a small rural town and being openly gay. Although she expressed the desire to dress in a more masculine way and cut her hair, she argued that she does not want any one to harass her family because of her actions and demeanor. Women in the charro cowboy community, as I will explain further, self regulate their behavior and the behavior of others. Veblen would have argued that this regulation of behavior can be viewed as an extension of the well-mannered leisure class. Homosexuality in the charro cowboy community is viewed as a violation of how young men and women should behave in public. Cielo stated that many older charro cowboy members expressed negative views about homosexuality despite greater acceptance in the wider Mexican society because they view it as an activity of lower class Mexicans.

Regulation of behavior is an essential component in maintaining the charro cowboy tradition. Even to generational charro cowboy female members, notions of charro cowboy respectability and tradition are regulated amongst themselves. While charro cowboy female members may recognize their own behavior contradicts the expectations of respectability, charro cowboy female members, in particular older women, are often regulated and managed by the criticism and stigmatization of others, usually targeting the behavior of younger women. Veblen explained that although women are in the subordinate and subservient role, within these secondary categories, a distinction is made between those individuals connected to noble and ignoble standing that can be understood on the basis of how women are categorized in the charro cowboy community. Since charro cowboy female members hold the hghest degree of honor, they must protect the status of other charro cowboy female members.

The protection of the status of a charro cowboy female member is usually controlled by older charro cowboy female members. In particular, older female family members play a crucial role in the manner in which female respectability is enacted, reproduced, and maintained. Married charro cowboy women, specifically, make sure to regulate inadequate or perceived deviant behavior. For example, Sofia, a 41-year-old with generational ties, often comments on how young women in the charro cowboy community must be corrected for their indecent behavior. Sofia stated, "If I see [a girl] doing something I think is incorrect, and I know their family, I wont allow it near me." Sofia specified that she will not condone behavior she deems to be inappropriate because such behavior reflects badly on the way that charro cowboy female members are treated. Manners are submerged in the ideals of respectability, therefore making deviation extremely visible. These acts of respectability, specific to the socialization of charro women and their normalized manners, act as an indication of their authentic membership. Sofia stated, "[The charro cowboys] only respect you if you respect yourself. If you do not respect yourself then they are not going to treat you properly." Therefore, charro cowboy female members must regulate each other and in particular, young charro cowboy female members, because their respectability and honor depend on it. Men in the charro cowboy community are not responsible for curtailing their harassment of women, but rather place blame on women who fail to respect their membership in the charro community through their manners and acts of respectability.

For example, during one particular *charreada*, Sofia and I witnessed a couple of young teenage girls hanging around with a couple of young charro cowboys. This group of charro cowboys appeared to be teenagers. Sofia recognized the young teenage girls as the daughters of a high-ranking official from the Mexican Federation of Charros. While Sofia was not related to them, she felt obligated to watch their behavior in order to assess whether she needed to step in and "control" the situation. The young charro cowboys, barely 18 themselves, belonged to the charro cowboy team that had preformed earlier in the day and were hanging out with the young girls during their time off. This was not uncommon, as many single (and married) charro cowboys frequently find themselves drinking and flirting with young women. An open bottle of tequila was hidden beside the one of the young charro cowboy's feet and was clearly being offered to the girls who were holding clear plastic cups tinted with the dark color of Coca Cola. Sofia had been watching the young girls for about an hour but did not realize that the girls were also watching her. When she was not looking they would pour tequila into their cups. Sofia interjected after she realized that one of the girls was getting tipsy and was "too flirtatious" around the young charro cowboys. She grabbed the girl by the arm and proceeded to order the other two girls to follow her away from the young charro cowboys. While the girls looked embarrassed, they did not fight Sofia and walked with her. Sofia grabbed a bottle of water from her purse and gave it to the girl that was intoxicated. She looked at her in the eye and sternly said, "If you do not give yourself value, they will never treat you right."

While this was most eventful example of an older charro cowboy female member reprimanding young girls with generational ties, older charro cowboy women, in particular mothers and grandmothers, often do not need to walk over to young women who are potentially risking their respectability. For example, charro cowboy female members often only need to look at a group of women with an obvious face of discontent in order to stop bad behavior. As I have previously mentioned, young charro cowboy women often recognize that they are being watched by other members of the community, both charro cowboy men and charro cowboy women. Therefore, young charro cowboy women will attempt to hide their inappropriate behavior but not always successfully. Older charro cowboy female members frequently stare and give looks of disapprobation. Their faces reveal enough of their discontent without having to walk over to the young charro cowboy women. This act of disapproval is enough to correct the behavior of young charro cowboy women without being verbally sanctioned.

In addition, older charro cowboy women often characterize the act of drinking or flirting with men as being lower class actions of promiscuous women. Veblen (1899) would characterize this behavior as an extension of how charro cowboy women utilize the invidious distinction placed upon them by their charro cowboy counterparts to maintain their status. Although charro cowboy female family members hold the most prestige in the ranking of women, they are still nowhere near the level of prestige as the men. Veblen (1899) stated, "The women, their occupations, their food and clothing, their habitual place in the house or village, and in extreme cases even their speech, become ceremonially unclean to the men." This ceremonially uncleanliness can be further extended if charro women fail to act respectably. This is why charro cowboy women are so invested in protecting and regulating the behavior of fellow charro cowboy women.

For example, Jacqueline, a 52-year-old charro cowboy woman with generational ties, on many occasions during *charreadas* will watch young charro cowboy women for acts of disobedience. She never leaves her spot in the audience but her obvious face of discontent is enough for a young charro cowboy girl to put down her drink and walk away. During one particular *charreada* in 2014, Jacqueline was watching a group of charro cowboys near the bull pins. This is a popular spot for younger charro cowboys, in particular charro cowboys with no generational ties, to drink, eat, smoke, and watch the *charreadas*. These spots are often very loud and draw the attention of the crowd. Two young charro cowboys signalled to young women who enthusiastically joined them. Jacqueline was uncomfortable with the young girls spending time with charro cowboys, but in particular, non-generational charro cowboys. According to Jacqueline, non-generational charro cowboys do not know how to respect charro cowboy female members because these men did not grow up in the charro cowboy community. Further, it is important to note that Jacqueline's concerns about the men are also racially motivated as the young charro cowboys were all men with indigenous ties and the young women were all lighter in complexion. The men's lower ranking status further threatened to contaminate the status of these young charro cowboy women. Jacqueline quickly sported a face of obvious disapproval. The young charro cowboy women made eye contact with Jacqueline and proceeded to leave the charro cowboy men. Jacqueline smiled at them because her plan had worked.

Jacqueline is a prime example of how older charro cowboy women manipulate and regulate the behavior of young charro cowboy women. While young charro cowboy women may find ways to resist and rebel against the highly restrictive belief system of the charro cowboy community, these young women still respect the authority of those women above them. They recognize that they have some power over them. This is the case even for young charro cowboy women who were once rebellious against the charro cowboy community. For example, Ana Cristiana has found herself now correcting the behavior of young charro cowboy women, despite her controversial past. Due to her background, Ana Cristiana stated that she is more aware of some of the mechanisms in which young girls hide their behavior from their watchful peers, making her even more conscious of potentially damaging behavior. Therefore, she is often the most critical of young charro cowboy girls and often reprimands them for drinking, smoking, and flirting with charro cowboy men of all ages.

Importantly, the process in which charro cowboy female members enact, reproduce, and maintain female charro cowboy respectability and honor is enforced by charro cowboy women and men. Since married charro cowboy women carry the highest prestige in the community, they find themselves trying to prove their worth and value continuously to others. Not because they want to, but rather because charro cowboys will not respect them unless they do. These acts include women recognizing their subservient role to charro cowboy men but also recognizing their superiority compared to other members of the community. Veblen stated:

> All the women in the group will share in the class repression and depreciation that belongs to them as women, but the status of women taken from hostile groups has an additional feature. Such a woman not only belongs to a subservient and low class, but she also stands in a special relation to her captor. She is a trophy of the raid, and therefore an evidence of exploit, and on this ground it is to her captor's interest to maintain a peculiarly obvious relation of mastery toward her.
>
> (Veblen 1899, 507)

Although charro cowboy women are not "taken" by the community, they do however represent this special feature that Veblen highlights above. Charro cowboy female family members hold a special relation to their charro cowboy husband, father, or grandfather. They are evidence of his success and their successful enactment of respectability and manners is a reflection of him. Further, since not all women in the charro cowboy community are regarded as equal, charro cowboy female members must protect their identities or face stigmatization from the community, in particular from their charro cowboy female peers. Although charro cowboy women recognize the underlining sexism and highly patriarchal nature of the community, many charro cowboy female family members would rather submit to the obvious gender inequality because inclusion in the charro cowboy tradition is better than potential exclusion. The consequences of violating these norms can lead to being expelled permanently from the charro cowboy community.

## Charro cowboy love interest

The process of courting is essential in the charro cowboy community. In particular, generational charro cowboy husbands and wives encourage their children to date and marry other generational charro cowboy community members in order to best maintain their traditions. Charro cowboy romances between men and women are also crucial components of the charro cowboy masculine identity as a charming "womanizer." Since a reputable charro cowboy female member holds the highest honor and prestige, charro cowboy love interests can serve as the next step into becoming an official high status charro cowboy wife. However, this is not always the case for young women (especially women who are not part of the community). While charro cowboy men have agency to experiment sexually with other women, charro cowboy female members are prohibited from such behaviour. There are two different subsets of charro cowboy love interests: 1) temporary charro cowboy love interests and 2) serious charro cowboy love interests. Serious love interests can be defined as women who charro cowboy men engage in long-term relationships with, the ultimate goal being marriage and children, while the temporary love interest involves no intention to permanently commit. Many charro cowboy women frame the second type as the charro cowboy man's "want to rid of his sexual need".

Charro cowboy love interests, whether they are serious or temporary love interests, aspire to have the presumed level of respect from the charro cowboy men that is bestowed upon charro cowboy wives. The status as charro cowboy wives is highly romanticized and many young girls are ignorant of the dynamics of this role. Charro cowboy wives, as well as other charro cowboy female family members, can be recognized as auxiliary members to charro cowboy men. Again, due to the highly patriarchal nature of the community, charro cowboy men are at the center of the community while women and are seen as dispensable. Charro cowboy love interests are viewed by charro cowboy men as fairly dispensable, but temporary love interests are classified as even more dispensable. Temporary charro cowboy love interests often preform a form of *vicarious prestige* due to the low status these women occupy without the association of charro cowboy men. According to Veblen, services or labor performed by subordinates (i.e. women in the community) is not for the aim of the self-actor but for their master (i.e. charro cowboy men). Veblen stated, "The leisure of the servant is not his own leisure. So far as he is a servant in the full sense, and not at the same time a member of a lower order of the leisure class proper, his leisure normally passes under the guise of specialized service directed to the furtherance of his master's fullness of life" (Veblen 1899, 29). While charro cowboy female family members, in particular wives, participate in vicarious leisure, I argue that charro cowboy love interests engage in *vicarious prestige*, ultimately connected with a charro cowboy's masculinity.

> Charro cowboy love interests, especially women without ties to the community, want to secure the respectability associated with being a charro cowboy wife. Being a charro cowboy love interest allows women to experience the short-term benefits of being a charro cowboy wife, thereby experiencing vicarious prestige. Vicarious prestige provides temporary love interests with some benefits of respectability because the charro cowboy man that has claimed her can protect her from other charro cowboy men. For example, Juana, a 22-year-old without any generational ties to the charro cowboy community, was the temporary love interest of Santiago. Santiago, a 23-year-old charro cowboy with generational ties, spotted Juana at a *charreada* during the summer of 2015. The following is

an extract from field notes collected on the day that they met:11:30AM The same people that I have seen at yesterday's charreada are here for the second installment of the competition series. The bar is open and older charro cowboys are already drinking and smoking their cigarettes on their horses. Juana is here with two other of her friends, Marissa and Camila. They are looking for charro cowboy boyfriends. They spent most of yesterday talking with charro cowboys and they are hoping today they will be able to continue to hang around with some of the charro cowboys they met. Juana is wearing a cowboy hat, cowboy boots, a belt with a metal buckle in the shape of a horse shoe, and a tank top. She is slender but her clothes fit tight enough to accentuate her curves. She stands out next to her friends because of her long brown hair that reaches the bottom of her back and her big bright brown eyes. Many charro cowboys watch her as she sits with her friends.

5:00PM Juana is a pretty girl from the town of Silao and was personally invited by the owner of the lienzo where the charreada is taking place. She mentions that her sister dated a charro cowboy from the neighboring town when she was younger. She describes how her sister was treated like a queen and was taken to many competitions. Juana likes being around horses and wants to be able to be a charro cowboy wife because she thinks only real men are charro cowboys even though she has no generational ties to the charro cowboys community.

7:00PM Juana watches the competition and watches a young Santiago from a distance. They make eye contact a few times and she occasionally smiles at him He notices her too.

7:30PM Santiago walks over to Juana who is sitting with her friends. He offers her a drink but only if she comes and sits with him and his charro cowboys team. He tells her how beautiful she is and that she is probably the most beautiful woman he has ever seen. Juana blushes and smiles as she agrees to walk over to other side of the lienzo. Her friends follow her and laugh about how Juana always gets charro cowboys to invite them for drinks. Juana takes a shot of tequila from the bottle and Santiago quickly pours her another drink. Her friends laugh and also join in.

10:00PM Juana is drunk along with Santiago who has been drinking since the early afternoon. A group of charro cowboy female family members a few feet away from them stare at her in disagreement. Santiago is now holding her close and places his hand around her waist. He attempts to give her a kiss but Juana refuses.

12:00AM Juana has stopped drinking for the night but disappears with Santiago. Marissa and Camila both tell me that she does this often with charro cowboy men. They are not worried but they say that she wont leave without them. Marissa states that Juana is having fun and that we should probably give her some space until she comes back.

1:00AM Juana resurfaces and is now ready to leave. She seems happy and is now sporting a hickey on both sides of her neck. Santiago is delighted and they exchange numbers. Juana asks him if she will see him tomorrow and he says yes. The girls leave. Santiago's Charro team laughs about his disappearance as they head over to their trucks and horses.

(Observation, July 2013)

Santiago never showed up to the *charreada* next morning. This is because Santiago treated Juana like a temporary charro cowboy love interest and not a charro cowboy female member. He knew that he was not returning to the competition but wanted Juana to still go in order to show her that he was still in charge of their "relationship". In my observations of these types of encounters, this was not uncommon. Juana's status as a non-generational admirer of the charro cowboy tradition further alienates her from the charro cowboy female respectability that she clearly wishes for from charro cowboy men. Juana wants to be a charro cowboy wife because she believes that charro cowboy men are the epitome of masculinity; however, Juana does not recognize that she functions as a tool to enhance Santiago's status rather than a tool to compliment his status. She was able to enjoy some of the benefits of being a respectable charro cowboy wife such as feeling special, but her inability to adhere to the rules and regulations about Charro cowboy female respectability leaves her vulnerable to deception and ultimately, disrespect.

Juana is a prime example of Veblen's understanding of the barbarian status of women. Veblen's conception of women as trophies is further explained in the following:

> At the same time, since his peculiar coercive relation to the woman serves to mark her as a trophy of his exploit, he will somewhat jealously resent any similar freedom taken by other men, or any attempt on their part to parade a similar coercive authority over her, and so usurp the laurels of his prowess, very much as a warrior would under like circumstances resent a usurpation or an abuse of the scalps or skulls which he had taken from the enemy.

> (Veblen 1899, 507)

Santiago was very strategic in making sure that everyone, both his charro cowboy teammates and her friends, knew that Juana was with him. He further placed his authority over her when he gave her two large hickeys on her neck before she left the *charreada* with her friends. Santiago and Juana are the prime example of the way that temporary charro cowboy love interests enact their barbaric and predatory habits.

Temporary charro cowboy love interests are often non-generational women who are fans of the charro cowboy tradition. They do not have the proper socialization to know what kind of situations will make them vulnerable to disrespect. In the case of Juana, her inability to restraint her perceived deviance (i.e. drinking in public with charro cowboy men) gave Santiago permission to treat Juana with less respect than someone who he classified as a charro cowboy female family member. Juana's mistakes were unbeknown to her and her friend group. Since Santiago continued to contact Juana for the next year when he was competing in Guanajuato, Juana did not see anything wrong in her actions. Juana's ultimate goal was to find a charro cowboy man to commit to her and she was more focused on making her relationship with Santiago a permanent situation. Although Santiago continued to contact Juana and meet with her when he visited her town, he was not exclusively seeing her. In fact, Santiago had an "on again, off again" girlfriend of three years named Olga. Olga, a 23-year-old with generational ties, is the niece of one of Santiago's teammates and can be classified as a charro cowboy female family member. Santiago's demeanor is not the same around Olga because the rules of respectability must be followed. Again, this is due to the possible consequences that Santiago will face if he disrespects Olga since charro cowboy female family members are protected by the community. Although Santiago is clearly cheating on Olga, his actions are not seen as deviant because most charro cowboy men also engage in extramarital affairs. Cheating is the fault of the women they choose to have these external relationships with because respectable women would refuse these advances.

Juana is considered a temporary love interest because her relationship with Santiago is not serious to him. She is not the only charro cowboy love interest to be led on by false hopes. Temporary love interests are often seduced by the romanticized ideals of rural masculinity such as perceived chivalry and are often drawn to the uniqueness of the charro cowboy tradition. As Juana had noted, she believed that "real men" are only found in the charro cowboy tradition. Her father is a wealthy businessman and had even offered to pay for Juana's college education. But, Juana was more focused on getting married than furthering her education. *Charreadas* are designed to place charro cowboy men in the center of the audience's focus and having a man dressed in charro cowboy attire can be presumed as advantageous for vicarious prestige. Although Mexico is shifting from the rural identities of the charro cowboy tradition, the symbolism, as previously mentioned, continues to make an impression in Mexican popular culture. Juana endures disrespect because she hopes that her idealized notions of the charro cowboy tradition will pay off. This however is not always the case.

Similar to Juana, Brenda once idealized charro cowboy men. She is now a 40-old divorcee with three children. Brenda has no generational ties to the charro cowboy tradition, and would attend competitions in Mexico City with her sisters. She met her ex-husband, Ruben, in the 1990s while he was competing in a regional competition. Ruben was a 40-year-old charro cowboy with generational ties and had to marry Brenda when they discovered that she was pregnant. Like Juana, Brenda was not familiar with the charro cowboy regulations in respects to female respectability and subsequently gained a reputation among the charro cowboy wives as a *zorra* or whore. Even though Brenda eventually became a charro cowboy wife, the other charro cowboy wives never truly accepted her because of her promiscuous past and her

inability to conform to their expectations. She did not know about her reputation among the charro cowboy female family members until she was married to Ruben. Although Brenda eventually married Ruben, she explained in
our conversations that Ruben did not want to commit to her and often would
date other women while they were together. She stated:

> [Ruben] does love women…(Laughs). That he did make clear from the
> beginning. He was a womanizer, with girlfriends, with fans… he felt spe-
> cial because we made him feel special…(pause) What I can say is that
> when we were together… together as [boyfriend and girlfriend], he was
> very [romantic] but when we got married… (pauses and then laughs) …
> he was a bastard.
>
> (Interview, 2013)

Brenda also stated that Ruben would write her love letters when they were
dating and he would always bring her flowers if he was in town. However, she
recalls these gestures as possibly strategic since Brenda would try to date
other men when Ruben would break up with her. Ruben felt some ownership
over Brenda, clearly what Veblen theorized as making a mark on her and
refusing other men to claim her. Brenda's distain for Ruben is centered on the
years of abuse that she underwent when they got married in the late 1990s
and his prolonged cycle of cheating. Her breaking point was after the birth of
her third child. Ruben became violent toward her and whipped her neck with
a rope that left a semi permanent mark. She told me that she sold everything
in their house while he was away competing so that he could not retaliate. She
lived in fear for several years however she now claims to feel free since Ruben
has now remarried with children. Brenda transitioned from a temporary
charro cowboy love interest to a charro cowboy wife after she got pregnant
with her first child out of wedlock and Ruben was pressured to marry her by
Brenda's family. Only a few people knew that Brenda was pregnant on her
wedding day due to the highly conservative nature of the charro cowboy
community. Her transition as a charro cowboy wife was not easy for her, but
while she was married she learned about the rules with respect to charro
cowboy female respectability through her mother-in-law, who did not care
that her son was physically abusive towards her.

While temporary charro cowboy love interests are usually treated as disposable, serious love interests are what one would consider to be the typical
courting scene. Temporary charro cowboy love interests often have no generational ties to the community and romanticize relationships with charro
cowboy men because they seek vicarious prestige from these relationships.
Although temporary love interests aspire to marriage, charro cowboy men do
not consider them viable options for marriage because they do not possess the
symbolic capital necessary for charro cowboy men to permanently commit to
their relationship. According to Pierre Bourdieu (1984), symbolic capital
refers to the degree of accumulated prestige, celebrity, consecration, or honor

that is founded on a dialectic of knowledge and recognition. Temporary love interests lack the socialization and education usually transmitted through the charro cowboy family, thus making relationships less likely to be permanent. Women categorized as temporary love interests often experience habitual disrespect from charro cowboy men.

Serious love interests, on the contrary, are predominantly women with generational ties to the community. These women are protected by the rules and regulations that must be adhered to by charro cowboy men in relation to charro cowboy female family members and outrank temporary love interests. Dating a woman with generational ties to the charro cowboy community consequently must lead to marriage. Charro cowboy men in the community desire their wives, in addition to being beautiful, to have generational ties to charro cowboy tradition because of the emphasis in the community on the progression of tradition. Charro cowboy men are more careful about being seen as deceptive by generational women since the ramifications can result in violence from her family.

The process of courtship in serious love interests follows strict rules. First, the charro cowboy man must try to attract a generational charro cowboy woman. These actions vary but revolve around three central themes: a) the charro cowboy's ability to impress charro cowboy women with their equestrian skills, b) their devotion to family, and c) their ability to respect them in public. Charro cowboy women are selective with regard to charro cowboy men since they have a reputation in the community as being womanizers. As mentioned earlier, the older generation of charro cowboy men compete for the continuity of the tradition while the younger generation of charro cowboy men compete for honor and prestige. In accordance with that pursuit of honor and prestige, the admiration of generational charro cowboy women further elevates their identities as charro cowboy men. They even had friendly competitions with each other to get the best girl in the crowd.

In my observations, I found that charro cowboy men who excelled during *charreadas* (i.e. got the most points from the judges) had the tendency to attract the most admirers, temporary or serious love interests. The *suertes* of the charro cowboy tradition are designed to demonstrate the power and ability of each individual competitor. When the competitor excels, he demonstrates strength, prowess, and most importantly, his masculinity. This is once more connected to the mode of predatory and barbaric habits expressed in sports. Veblen stated, "They not only improve the contestant's physique, but it is commonly added that they also foster a manly spirit, both in the participants and the spectators" (Veblen 1899, 199). Contemporary studies on organized sport have examined the mechanisms in which sports bolsters a sagging ideology of male superiority and helps to reconstitute masculine hegemony (Bryson 1987; Hall 1988; Kimmel 1987; Messner, 1989; 1990; Theberge 1981). Women in the charro cowboy community are attracted to the characteristics expressed by men in the community because hypermasculine traits are held in high esteem. Charro cowboy men who excel in the *charreadas* are as a result considered to be the most desirable by both temporary and serious love interests.

Serious love interests, due to the rules of charro cowboy female respectability, are limited in the manner in which they can approach charro cowboy men while temporary love interests experience no such thing. Hence, when a serious love interest wants to demonstrate to the charro cowboy man that she is interested, she will make eye contact with him to indicate that he can approach her. For example, Yessica, a generational charro cowboy wife with two children, described her relationship with her husband prior to their marriage. She stated that she did not make the first move because she did not want him to think she was not a respectable woman or sexually promiscuous. Yessica stated, "I would look at him and smile. He knew that I liked him." Eye contact, in this context, is significant to display interest and a smile gives the charro cowboy man the authorization to approach the potential serious love interest. The following observation in Mexico City exemplifies the use of eye contact and smiling in the charro cowboy community:

Erika,[2] a 27-year-old with generational ties, is sitting with her two female cousins, her mother, and her aunt. They are there to watch her father compete in the *charreada*. She is sitting next to her cousin, Priscilla, and commenting on the competition They make note of who they know but also general gossip about members of the charro cowboy team. Her father is competing against a second-rate team from a town outside of Mexico City. This team is relatively young and is funded by a charro cowboy jefe who never comes to competitions. Erika notices Oscar, a charro cowboy completo, who is performing the manganas de pie with his team. Oscar is a generational charro cowboy and has been to several competitions in Mexico City throughout his career. He is 29 and is very popular among charro cowboy women and fans. Erika watches as Oscar perfectly carries out each mangana de pie, a very difficult task to complete. His first attempt is flawless in technique and he receives praise from the audience, including Erika. Erika comments to Priscilla on how attractive Oscar looks competing. They laugh after Priscilla says, "Especially his butt in those pants!" Oscar concentrates on his last attempt and successfully performs the hardest method of success, "el orcado" or "the hanged man". "The hanged man" calls for the charro cowboy man to launch the rope at the legs of a mare and then use the weight of his own body to flip the horse in mid-stop. This particular maneuver is called "the hanged man" because those who incorrectly execute this *suerte* run the risk of accidently hanging themselves when the horse's feet latch onto the rope. Therefore, the perfect execution of this method is rendered impressive and highlights the skills, strength, and professionalism of the charro cowboy man. Erika, clearly impressed with his work, was able to make eye contact with Oscar and smiled at him from her seat in the audience. Oscar quickly noticed her, since she was a well-recognized charro cowboy female family member from the association hosting the event. Oscar smiled back to her and tipped his sombrero at her direction. Priscilla quickly said, "Viste eso! (Did you see that!) Erika had opened the door for further interaction with Oscar.

(Observation, May 2013)

Erika, being an attractive woman, has no trouble drawing the attention of charro cowboy men. As stated, she is a generational woman and her father is a highly recognized charro cowboy competitor in the community. At 27, Erika is a seasoned beauty contestant and is a former charro cowboy queen of her father's team. Erika's interest in Oscar is centered on his skills and confidence. Later that evening, Oscar approached Erika by greeting her mother, aunt, and two cousins. He made sure to be polite and to adhere to the rules of respectability by not asking Erika to drink with him. Erika and Oscar were able to talk about the *charreada* while not risking Erika's status as a respectable charro cowboy female family member. This does not mean that Erika will never drink with Oscar, however their first encounters require some regulation and strategic maneuvering in order to solidify Erika's status as a serious charro cowboy love interest. In this scenario, Oscar clearly displayed his intentions as serious rather than temporary.

According to Noel F. McGinn's (1966) analysis of marriage and family in middle-class Mexico, *noviazgo* or dating is an essential period for young Mexican women to pay attention to their boyfriends. McGinn stated:

> Tradition states that the language and music of courtship used by the suitor should be rich with reference to her beauty and the great need he has for her. Furthermore, all this passionate wooing is to occur without the young woman's having to worry about being compromised, for she should always be accompanied by a chaperone... If he observes traditional rules, there are few opportunities for a young middle-class man physically to demonstrate his affection for his [girlfriend].
>
> (McGinn 1966, 306)

Although McGinn (1966) examined family and marriage dynamics nearly 51 years ago, the traditional dynamics are still applicable to the charro cowboy tradition and what I have theorized with Veblen's work. Charro cowboy men, as I have argued, with great frequency reference the beauty of both temporary and serious love interest, yet serious love interests periodically require chaperones. Beauty is essential because it is not defined by the love interests, but rather by the charro cowboy men. Veblen stated, "Men who are trained in predatory ways of life and modes of thinking come by habituation to apprehend this form of the relation between sexes as good and beautiful" (Veblen 1899, 507). Charro cowboys often place more value upon beautiful respectable charro cowboy female members. Their predatory habits are focused more upon what their mastery and coercion over women means for them.

In case of Erika and Oscar, their initial encounter was witnessed by Erika's family members, but I had the unique opportunity to observe their relationship unfold in my initial study of the charro cowboy community in 2013. Erika continued to attend *charreadas* with her family and Oscar would occasionally show up to competitions where Erika's father would be competing. Oscar would always greet Erika and he would sit with her family members.

This continued for about a month until Oscar finally asked Erika on a date in August of 2013. While I was not present for their date, Erika reported that Oscar took her to his family member's *quinceañera* and invited her cousins to come along. Her cousins served two functions. First, as Erika and Oscar's official chaperone, hence limiting any inappropriate forms of physical affection. Second, Oscar's invitation established him as a charro cowboy man devoted to family and charro cowboy traditions. During her date, Erika was able to learn more about Oscar's family and his values without comprising her own. Erika was fairly interested in Oscar and their relationship was formally defined a week later as exclusive. This was due to Oscar's ability to impress Erika with his charro cowboy skills, demonstrate devotion to family, and treat her with respect.

As a formal couple, Erika made sure to establish her claim on Oscar during *charreadas*. Again, due to Oscar's talents as a charro cowboy, he was very popular among serious and temporary love interests. In the following year, Erika and Oscar were still dating but Erika revealed that the "honeymoon phase" of their relationship was over. Even after a year, Oscar still adhered to the regulations of charro cowboy female respectability. Thus, he honored Erika by remaining faithful to her throughout their relationship and no longer messaging or talking to potential love interests. Erika's role as a serious love interests requires her active participation in maintaining her status as a serious love interest with the expectation of marriage. She is expected to oversee or manage Oscar's behavior in order to protect her goals. For example, Erika would scare away temporary love interests that would try to gain the attention of her boyfriend. In one instance, Erika stared at women who would linger near Oscar and when she was with her friends, they would also help her by making temporary love interests uncomfortable with their "dirty looks". Erika stated that these mechanisms of stigmatization were essential in protecting her boyfriend from temporary love interests that may "throw themselves at him". It became her "job" to protect her relationship from potential threats.

In the summer of 2015, Erika and Oscar got engaged. Although engaged, Oscar admitted that he still talked to a few temporary charro cowboy love interests. Erika knew about Oscar's infidelity but was still adamant about getting married to Oscar. A charro cowboy wedding and marriage would solidify her position as a charro cowboy wife, placing her at the top of the social hierarchy. Serious love interests are socialized to accept infidelity and violence in their relationships as long as outsiders are not aware of it. Erika refused to talk about Oscar's infidelity but her friends were open to the conversation. They mentioned that Oscar was rumored to see women when he was out of town but Erika did not care as long as she had the promise of permanent commitment. Erika was more involved with planning her wedding than regulating the behavior of her fiancé.

Further, a charro cowboy wedding is a high prestige act that evokes all the symbolism of the charro cowboy tradition to solidify a women's status in the community. Women wear the traditional white dress but incorporate elements of the charro cowboy tradition in how the wedding party is dressed and how they arrive with the groom at the ceremony. Charro cowboy husbands-to-be dress in charro cowboy gala attire or a fancier form of the traditional charro cowboy attire to celebrate their position as charro cowboy husbands. Having a charro cowboy wedding that incorporates the charro cowboy tradition has become another component of the charro cowboy leisure class. As previously stated, the charro cowboy leisure class is the wealthier and more honor focused in the charro cowboy community. Erika can use her charro cowboy wedding to display wealth but also use the tradition to elevate her prestige in the community.

Ultimately, the serious charro cowboy love interest endures disrespect through infidelity and violence but will endure such problems in order to maintain their status as honorable and respectable women. Revealing or confronting problems of infidelity and violence makes them vulnerable to public disrespect not just by charro cowboy men, but also charro cowboy women. The high ranking charro cowboy family members practice a culture of silence that encourages women to never address domestic issues. Serious love interests are encouraged to never fight or resist their future husband's demands. Therefore, serious love interests are conditioned to be satisfied with infidelity as long as they are the most serious love interest and their ultimate goal of marriage has not been compromised. Issues of domestic violence are not frequently discussed but the older generation of charro cowboy wives have discussed their experiences because younger women were more aware of outsiders who report issues of domestic violence to the police. Julia, aged 71, faced constant violence through her marriage to her charro cowboy husband. During her interview, Julia disclosed how her late husband would beat her for not cooking the right meal and his anger was heightened by his alcoholism. Her most horrifying story was about enduring violence during her second pregnancy. Julia described how she was kicked repeatedly in the stomach by her late husband because of her alleged flirtatious behavior with the bakery owner. She also recalls her husband coming home from the ranch and shooting his gun at lamp posts when he became irate. Although he never shot her or pointed the gun at her, she said that she would often hide under her bed when he came home drunk. While Julia's experiences are the most severe examples, they depict a common narrative about jealousy and violence. Julia never divorced her charro cowboy husband because divorce would lead to her permanent exclusion by the community and her parents at the time would never have accepted her return home. Further, she never reported her abuse to the authorities because she said, "You just don't do that".

In the context of a hypermasculine culture like the charro cowboy community, domestic violence is still a problem for some cowboy families. Serious love interests, unlike temporary love interests, are more likely to experience these forms of abuse because of the longevity of romantic relationships. This violence and disrespect is an unfortunate consequence of the charro cowboy's barbaric and predatory habits that exploits women. Temporary love interests may be subjected to continuous disrespect, but since their interactions with charro cowboy men tend to expire rapidly, they are not subjected to these forms of physical submission. Serious love interests, as mentioned earlier, are placed in a position where the transition from romantic courtship is short-lived but infidelity will be endured as long as the couple is engaged and married. While some serious love interests aspire to marry, there are obviously a few women who grow tired of charro cowboy men. These generational charro cowboy women will sometimes date an outsider of the community but will eventually find that dating men in the community is more feasible. Serious love interests have complained that other Mexican men outside of the charro cowboy community do not place value on tradition, making it hard to maintain a serious relationship with them. Although some serious love interests may desire the resolution of infidelity and violence, there are few opportunities to combat these problems in the charro cowboy community. In addition, women who do wish to escape find little help within the community to escape unfaithful or violent charro cowboy men.

## The invisible women of the charro cowboy tradition

*Las vendedoras* or sales women of the charro cowboy community are the lowest ranking women of the charro cowboy community. These women are practically invisible to charro cowboy men because they are not part of the charro cowboy tradition or adoring fans. These women are usually the vendors focused on their businesses. While not all charro cowboy men treat *vendedoras* like they are not present, the majority of charro cowboy men, in particular, the older generation do not engage with these women in the same manner that they engage with charro cowboy female family members or love interests. Because the charro cowboy tradition is culturally socialized from birth, charro cowboy men have "learned" how to interact with *vendedoras*. They are never rude but do not pay them much attention. These women are responsible for providing food, for a reasonable price of course, making drinks, selling handmade charro cowboy accessories, etc. These women are not always alone but are accompanied by their young children and sometimes their husbands or male family members. It is significant to note that the 90% of these *vendedoras* are of indigenous origin. Therefore, they are darker in complexion, may dress in simpler clothing, and have no generational connection to the charro cowboy tradition. These women and their families take advantage of the capitalistic opportunity at *charreadas*, knowing that charro cowboys get hungry and thirsty or need to replace charro cowboy equipment.

The most prestigious *charreadas* such as the championship or major qualifying regional competitions regulate the *vendadoras* that are allowed in the *lienzo* arena. But, many *vendadoras* can be found outside the competition. Due to who the Mexican Federation of Charros allows to sell food, drinks, and items at championship or major qualifying regional competitions, these major competitions have fewer traditional vendors than smaller competitions in other places throughout Mexico. Championship series and major qualifying regional competitions tend to have vendors that are connected to the charro cowboy *jefes* that were discussed earlier. *Vendadoras* are usually poor or working class Mexican women who do not have connections or networks in the Mexican Federation of Charros. *Vendadoras*, nevertheless, are a significant component of the hierarchy of charro cowboy women.

*Vendadoras* are not formally considered to be charro cowboy women or in the charro cowboy tradition, they are the lowest ranking women in comparison with the women present at competitions. Unlike charro cowboy love interests, *vendadoras* do not necessarily want to be charro cowboy wives or desire to be in the tradition. Their main objective is to make money. While *vendadoras* can become charro cowboy love interests, if they are young and considered beautiful by charro cowboy men, they are never considered as serious love interests. They are sometimes even joked about when charro cowboy men want to make fun of each other. Charro cowboy men interact with *vendadoras* when necessary but most of the interactions that *vendadoras* have with members of the charro cowboy community are with higher ranking women. According to Veblen, those who perform low status or less honorable work are often separated from those who are perceived to perform high status or honorable work. Therefore, charro cowboy men usually have their ranch hands or ranch assistants get them food from the *vendadoras*. Ranch hands or ranch assistants, as mentioned previously, are usually poor and of indigenous origin and therefore share the same class and ethnic backgrounds.

*Vendadoras* find most charro cowboy men to be condescending and elitist. Regardless of the types of discrimination that they personally face, *vendadoras* are in a unique position to see the contradictions within the charro cowboy community that are often ignored within the charro cowboy community (i.e. issues of classism, racism, sexism, etc.). The invisibility of *vendadoras* to charro cowboy men allows them to observe the behavior of charro cowboy men with other people. For example, Pati is a 40-old *vendadoras* who travels to different *charreadas* in central Mexico. Pati sells *comida rapida* or Mexican fast food like tacos, quesadillas, and gorditas of various meats. She sells her delicious food at a reasonable price and has been going to *charreadas* for about 15 years. *Charreadas* are the perfect setting for Pati to make money to bring back to her family of four. Her husband sometimes joins her if she requires additional help but the majority of help is provided by her mother and two sons. Pati has always has been an entrepreneur in Mexico City but found that the charro cowboy community can a perfect place to sell food above the average rate. Many of the *charreadas* are located away from other food venues, therefore making Pati and several other *vendedoras* the only options.

Since Pati has been working at *charreadas*, she has seen changes in the community that are often mentioned by the older generation of charro cowboys. She states:

You did not see the advertising or the need for better...better audio. It is all changing... changing fast. The charro cowboys look more nervous, less relaxed than when I started. The looked worried...especially the young ones. It used to be about family but I see it changing.

(Interview, June 2013)

Pati recognizes the changes in charro cowboy men with the impact of the standardization of the Mexican Federation of Charros. Further, she recognizes that younger charro cowboys seem more nervous and are less likely to relax in these spaces. She states that charro cowboys do not really make eye contact with her if they are buying their own food. Pati explained that most of the men she has conversations with are charro cowboy workers or charro cowboy rookies. When her husband occasionally helps her, charro cowboy men do talk to him but she believes that this is because he is a man and they respect him more than her. This is not surprising when one realizes that charro cowboy workers and charro cowboy rookies have similar backgrounds.

Another *vendedoras*, Monse, workers for a tequila business that is owned by a charro cowboy *jefe*. Monse is 30 years old and is a resident of Guadalajara, Jalisco. She had only been working for this business for four months when I interviewed her in 2013. Similar to Pati, Monse is of a darker complexion, bigger build, and has two children. Her husband is an alcoholic and therefore she has to work to support her two children. She was referred to this job by her brother who is a charro cowboy rookie working for a charro cowboy *jefe*. Monse's job requires her to sell alcoholic beverages such as bottles or shots of tequila, whiskey, or rum, *micheladas* (a Mexican drink prepared with beer, lime juice, assorted sauces, species, and peppers), a variety of Mexican beers, non-alcoholic drinks (soda and water), and Marlboro cigarettes. There are a few different stands around the *lienzo* that sell drinks to the public, but Monse's stand is located right behind the area where charro cowboy gather. Unlike Pati, Monse deals with charro cowboys, especially the older generation of charro cowboys since they tend to drink throughout the day at *charreadas*. She also reported that they do not make eye contact with her but will always hassle her for more drinks. Although she has told various charro cowboys her name, she is only referred to as *muchacha* or young lady. This is a mechanism that creates distance between charro cowboys and *vendedoras*, highlighted by Veblen's conception of invidious distinction between people.

*Vendedoras* recognize that they are ignored by the charro cowboy community. Many state that they enjoy the music and believe it is a really beautiful tradition, but they do not feel like they are included in the celebrations. They recognize their position as workers or servers. This is once again Veblen's argument about barbaric and predatory habits that create distinctions among individuals. Restating Veblen's point, "The first requisite of a good servant is that he should conspicuously know his place" (Veblen 1899, 29). The pattern of subordination of individuals that are not in the charro cowboy tradition based on class, gender, and ethnic origin becomes evident. *Vendedoras* rank the lowest in the hierarchy of charro cowboy women. Although they may not be formally involved in the charro cowboy tradition or have generational ties to the community, *vendedoras* take part in the major work of elevating the status of charro cowboy men. Similar to charro cowboy female members and charro cowboy love interests (both serious and temporary), the interactions between *vendedoras* and charro cowboy men allows them to feel powerful, important, and honorable compared to those they perceive as being beneath them. The charro cowboy community no longer holds the same welcoming character and has allowed the barbaric and predatory habits of exploitation, invidious distinction, and subornation of others to contaminate its peaceable origins.

When asking charro cowboy men about *vendedoras* many of them could not recall significant interactions with them. Again, this is due to the fact that they do not interact with them and prefer to get someone else to order their food or get them a drink. However, charro cowboy rookies, in particular those with indigenous ties and modest backgrounds, did report positive interactions with *vendedoras*. Miguel, a 20-year-old charro cowboy rookie, said that *vendedoras* were often the only positive interactions they had at *charreadas*. Due to the classist and racist tendencies of generational charro cowboys, charro cowboy rookies will find these *vendedoras* and the spaces they work in function like sanctuaries from the continuous discrimination. Miguel states that he enjoys eating tacos and talking to the women who make them. Sometimes charro cowboy rookies even know their family members or find some familial ties. But, charro cowboy rookies that have been participating in the community for longer periods of time recognize that there is a division between *vendedoras* and the rest of the charro cowboy community. They begin to slowly pull away in order to adapt to the norms of the traditions and the expectations for charro cowboy men. Pati mentioned that she witnessed this particular type of behavior from many charro cowboy rookies that she met over time. She stated,

> They were always smiling and talking to [my family]. Over the years, they would only spend five minutes of their time. It is sad but it is normal. I do not expect them to be [eating] next to me (laughs). They would tell me about the [charro cowboy men] ...you know, the ones with grey in their beard...and say "Oh they treat me like shit" or "He hates me". It is sad to hear but they love being a charro cowboy more. (sighs) I only make their food...(laughs)... I am not their mother.
>
> (Interview, 2013)

Pati acknowledges that over time charro cowboy rookies modify their behavior around them. Although she tried to make her comments humorous, she was noticeably hurt by these changes.

*Vendedoras* may be the lowest ranking women in the community but they are the most aware of the issues of the community. The hold what W.E.B. Du

Bois (1903) regarded as double consciousness characterizing the internal conflict of subordinated groups in an oppressive society. This is due to their lack of membership in the charro cowboy community. Their interactions in the community are limited and are only at *charreadas*. They are not integrated in the community like charro cowboy female family members nor do they desire to be included like temporary love interests. Their goal in life is to make a profit so they can go home and feed their family. They do not have to accept their subordination like charro cowboy female family members and charro cowboy love interests because they have the option to leave. Many *vendedoras* do in fact take their business elsewhere if they feel like they cannot deal with the lack of eye contact or invisibility. If they leave the charro cowboy community, they are not ostracized because to many it is like they were never there.

In conclusion, the ranking of women in the charro cowboy community yields an important argument about the barbarian status of women in barbaric and predatory cultures. While the charro cowboy community holds many peaceable elements, the exploitation and use of women clearly demonstrates why Veblen's work holds value in this ethnographic assessment. The distinction between temporary and serious charro cowboy love interests resonates with the charro cowboy's inability to respect women who "do not respect themselves". Charro cowboy female members have to engage in reputation management. Temporary love interests lack the necessary socialization to avoid stigmatization and they are often used to demonstrate charro cowboy prowess and the ability to "satisfy their needs". Love is complex in the charro cowboy community and it is often romanticized, but there are serious issues of domestic violence and emotional abuse. Charro cowboy wives are expected to remain devoted to their husbands while some exercise the freedom to explore other sexual relationships. *Vendedoras*, although the lowest ranked of all the charro cowboy women, are essential in understanding the social dynamics between charro cowboys and the women they perceive invisible. They are the silent watchers and the most informed of charro cowboy drama.

## Notes

1  My initial examination of the charro cowboy community pertained to their gendered division of labor. In this work, I theorized the concept of *hacienda culture* as a subset of traditionalist masculinity due to the distinctive notions and definitions of masculinity that resonate with the charro cowboy community's history. I argued that charro cowboys that actively participate in the community reject emerging egalitarian perceptions of gender ideology distinct from their own. By adopting *hacienda culture*, charro cowboys reproduce and maintain traditionalist gender ideologies in their families and romantic relationships (Marquez, 2016). This work is separate from my analysis here.

2  Erika first mistook my involvement in the charro cowboy community as looking for boyfriends because she thought I was interested in Oscar. I had interviewed him the previous day and therefore Erika thought that I was interested in pursuing him. Once I revealed to her the indications of my observations and interviews, she was more at ease with telling me the story of her romance with Oscar and her involvement in the charro cowboy community.

# References

Bourdieu, Pierre. *Distinction: A Social Critique of the Judgement of Taste*. London: Routledge & Kegan Paul. 1984.

Bryson, Lois. "Sport and the maintenance of masculine hegemony." *Women's Studies International Forum*, vol. 10 (1987): 349–360.

Du Bois, W. E. B. *The Souls of Black Folk; Essays and Sketches*. Chicago: A. G. McClurg, 1903. New York: Johnson Reprint Corp. 1968.

Hall, M. Ann. "The Discourse of Gender and Sport: From Femininity to Feminism." *Sociology of Sport Journal*, vol. 5, no. 4 (December 1988): 330–340.

Kimmel, Michael. *Changing men: New directions in research on men and masculinity*. Thousand Oaks: Sage Publications. 1987.

Marquez, Beatriz A."The Effects of Hacienda Culture on the Gendered Division of Labor within the Charro Community." *Gender Issues* (2016): 1–20.

McGinn, Noel F. "Marriage and Family in Middle-Class Mexico." *Journal of Marriage and Family*, vol. 28, no. 3 (August 1966): 305–313.

Messner, Michael. "Masculinities and Athletic Careers," *Gender and Society* (December 1989).

Messner, Michael. "Masculinities and Athletic Careers." *Gender and Society* (December: "When bodies are weapons: Masculinity and violence in Sport") *International Review for the Sociology of Sport* (September 1990).

Seed, Patricia. *To love, honor, and obey in colonial Mexico: Conflicts over marriage choice, 1574–1821*, Stanford, California: Stanford University Press, 1988.

Theberge, Nancy. "A Critique of Critiques: Radical and Feminist Writings on Sport." *Social Forces*, Vol. 60, no. 2 (December 1981): 341–353.

Veblen, Thorstein. "The Barbarian Status of Women". *American Journal of Sociology*, vol. 4, no. 4 (1899): 503–514.

Veblen, Thorstein. *The Theory of the Leisure Class: An Economic Study of Institutions*. New York: Reprint by The New American Library. 1953[1889].

# 5 Beautiful women on horses

While some women in the charro cowboy community do not wish to participate in the charro cowboy competitions, there are those who have fought for the right to do so. *Escaramuzas* can be defined as a type of all female equestrian drill team with musical accompaniment linked to the historical significance of the charro cowboy tradition (Sands 1993). In the community, *escaramuzas* refers to a group of women who demonstrate their horsemanship skills by preforming daring and risky synchronized precision horse ballets. These women typically wear colorful traditional garments and ride side saddle. They are usually from respectable and wealthy charro cowboy families in the community since becoming an *escaramuza* requires a sizeable monetary investment due to the expense of specialized saddles, garments, and so on. Comparable to the historical social circumstances that link modern charro cowboys to the charro cowboys of the colonial and post-colonial period, *escaramuzas* also make up an integral part of the community due to their revolutionary predecessors who fought side by side with charro cowboy men during the wars of Mexican Independence and their outfits commemorate those women. However, *escaramuzas* did not have the support of either the government or the Mexican Federation of Charros until 1992. *Escaramuzas* also lack agency to make decisions within the Mexican Federation of Charros and are denied the opportunity to hold leadership positions within the organization because they have no voting rights. Their presence at these meetings is merely symbolic.[1]

Kathleen Sands stated, "Though charro teams express great pride in the *escaramuzas* who ride with their associations and strive to support and encourage them, they see their own competition as significantly more important than the women's riding demonstration and retain the power to decide when and where the *Escaramuzas* will perform and their place in the *charreada* schedule" (Sands 1993, 163). The inclusion of *escaramuzas* in *charreadas* was strategic because it is also linked to the charro cowboy business principles: additional costs can be billed to charro cowboy teams with a partnering *escaramuza* team. While charro cowboy men assert a specific type of Mexican rural masculinity, *escaramuzas* provide *charreadas* with a feminine touch that many charro cowboys see as necessary and that is also specific to Mexican rural femininity. Further, *escaramuza* teams are pertinent to the charro cowboy leisure class due to the financial demand to fund them and charro cowboy *jefes* can further demonstrate their visible success with their ability to spend money. Some Charro teams even elect an *escaramuza* as their team's queen further exhibiting the barbaric and predatory cultural habits of the charro cowboy community that place women as mere tools for additional prestige. The Mexican Federation of Charro cowboys also elects an *escaramuza* queen every several years to represent the community in prestigious and notable *charreadas*.

In this chapter, I argue that women who compete as *escaramuzas* tend to be wealthy, have generational ties, and are seen as respectable members of the charro cowboy community compared to other women. Within the hierarchy of charro cowboy women, they tend to be charro cowboy female family members, yielding a particular sect of respectability and prestige (see Chapter 4 for details). I examine *escaramuzas* as a separate component in *charreadas*, how they view themselves, and how charro cowboy men view them. Yet, their participation and competitions are, nevertheless, secondary to charro cowboy men, regardless of how skilled these women may be. In addition, I will analyse their status with the Mexican Federation of Charros to illustrate that their role in the charro cowboy community remains symbolic even though charro cowboy women have played a crucial role in charro cowboy history.

## The duplication of the Spanish aristocracy

*Charreadas* are centered on the participation of the charro cowboy men who complete the *suertes charras* or the charro cowboy events. Like the charro cowboy man, the *escaramuza* has a historical past bounded to Spanish colonialism and revolutionary resistance of tyrannical power. The word *escaramuza* in English translates to skirmish or an episode of irregular or unpremeditated fighting, especially between small or outlying elements of armies or fleets (Sands 1993). The very name highlights the fighting and predatory characteristics illustrated in the charro cowboy tradition's history. Although charro cowboy women were originally of humble socio-economic backgrounds, the presidency of Porfirio Diaz in the late 1870s presented the potential for aristocratic women to appropriate the charro cowboy tradition. This appropriation shifted what Veblen (1899) would consider, the peaceable traits of the *escaramuza* iconography to an iconography centered in conspicuous consumption. Sands argued:

> In the New World, aristocratic women continued to be trained in the Spanish equestrian tradition, but with the development of ranching and the civil wars in Mexico, women took on roles as stock handlers, couriers, and fighting, adopting a much more active riding style in process. Although the term *escaramuza,* which means "skirmish," suggests this later mode of riding, the charreada *escaramuza* preserves the appearance

of the genteel seventeenth-, eighteenth-, and nineteenth-century tradition in its use of sidesaddle, graceful protocols, and costume. While colorful and ornate, the dresses the girls wear are modestly high-necked and long-sleeved, and skirts come no more than two inches above the boot tops. Pantaloons and crinolines ensure modesty as well, and the full costume and sidesaddle technique give the charras an air of aristocratic grace that masks their physical exertion and daring.

(Sands 1993, 11)

*Escaramuzas* represent the clash between the Mexican women of the past with a fighting and work ethos and the respectable equestrian traditions of Spanish European society. While the origins of *escaramuzas* are bounded by class and ethnic distinctions made by Spanish colonization and notions of decency, the modern *escaramuza* emulates these notions of aristocratic decency and femininity more than the historical past of the lower classes. As previously argued in Chapter 3, female respectability plays an essential part in the ranking of women in the charro cowboy community and *escaramuzas* are no different. Their performance is the public display of these notions of decency, grace, and modesty that was borrowed from Spanish notions of class. It is evident that the performance of *escaramuzas* is another contradiction to the charro cowboy beliefs regarding the subject of class, gender, and ethnic origin. Further, *escaramuzas* are an important tool in the conspicuous consumption of the charro cowboy leisure class.

While the equestrian style is borrowed from the colonial Spanish aristocracy, the outfits that *escaramuzas* compete in are borrowed by the Adelita style of dress. The Adelita dress was made famous by the heroines of the revolution. According to Sands, "Adelita is a legendary figure said to have a friend and companion to Pancho Villa early in his career as a general. She also gained fame as a fighter in his army. Her costume—a long skirt, *rebozo* [cloth garment] crossed over her bodice, and calf-length boots—became popular with women during the revolution" (Sands 1993, 158). The use of the Adelita style of dress demonstrates the juxtaposition of Spanish aristocratic notions of decency and the low class symbols of the revolutionary women of Mexico. This is a way in which *escaramuzas* romanticize the charro cowboy women that fought alongside men during the Mexican civil wars. This romanticized notion of the *escaramuza* does not benefit the women who enact its significance, but rather the very charro cowboy men who fund their participation.

The historical significance of the *escaramuzas* has been investigated by various scholars across different disciplines (Valero Silva 1989; Nájera-Ramírez 1994, 1996, 2000, 2002, 2003; Sands 1993; López 1997; Chávez Torres 1998; Ancona 1999; Montfort 2007; Ramírez Barreto 2009; Miranda 2013; Medina 2015). While it is understood that *escaramuzas* are pivotal to the history of the charro cowboy tradition, I argue, using the Veblen (1899) theoretical framework, women who compete in charro cowboy competition as *escaramuzas* are wealthier than ever before and come from highly respectable generational Charro families. I further argue that *escaramuzas* can be best understood through the theorization of Veblen's conception of conspicuous consumption since the performance of *escaramuzas* is evidence of wealth of both their families and the people that fund them. The financial burden of competing *escaramuza* is similar to that of charro cowboy men. However, the financial burden has become even more evident in the last two decades according to active competing *escaramuzas*. This financial burden limits participation to only the upper class charro cowboy community because *escaramuza* teams must have matching dresses, boots, sombreros, boots, bows, saddles, riding sticks, spurs, etc. that are highly costly for a team of eight. There is no room for individuality in the realm of *escaramuzas* because their purpose is to perform in unison and display their beauty and grace.

The ability to compete in the charro cowboy community as an *escaramuza* is limited to the wealthy. The many *escaramuzas* that I interviewed described the costs as high but worth it in order to be included in *charreadas*. For Cielo, the 27-year-old closet lesbian, competing as an *escaramuza* for a well known team gives her a sense of pride. While Cielo may have ulterior motives for competing as an *escaramuza* (to prevent her reputation being questioned by others in the charro cowboy community), Cielo's family is also wealthy enough to finance her continued participation. Her mother was an *escaramuza* in the 1980s and competed in various parts of Mexico. It was assumed that Cielo would also participate as an *escaramuza* alongside her mother. Cielo has been competing professionally since she was eight years old. Unlike charro cowboy teams where most of the participants are 18 or older, *Escaramuza* teams vary in age. Some *Escaramuza* teams can compete in juvenile competitions where the participants are under the age of 18, the majority of *escaramuza* festivals have participant of various ages. The purpose of these performances is to present the notions of decency, grace, and modesty that epitomize charro cowboy female respectability. Cielo is able to feel included in the charro cowboy tradition without resisting the socio-cultural structure.

As a wealthier family in the charro cowboy community, participation in the *escaramuza* competitions is an evidence of wealth and prestige. Veblen (1899) argued that activities in peaceable society are the minimum required for subsistence and physical efficiency. As society becomes contaminated with more predatory and barbaric habits, consumption moves beyond the minimum requirements of subsistence and exceeds the standards of survival. Veblen argued:

> Conspicuous consumption of valuable goods is a means of reputability to the gentleman of leisure. As wealth accumulates on his hands, his own unaided effort will not avail to sufficiently put his opulence in evidence by this method. The aid of friends and competitors is therefore brought in by resorting to the giving of valuable presents and expensive feasts and entertainments.
>
> (Veblen 1899, 36)

Value is placed on the reputability that the participation of these activities provides to the leisure class. *Escaramuzas* provide respectability for the people that fund their performances in addition to providing families and charro cowboy *jefes* with prestige and honor. Since *escaramuzas* are a tool of conspicuous consumption, participation has to be reserved for individuals who can yield a positive reputation for the charro cowboy leisure class.

Cielo understands that being an *escaramuzas* is not for everyone. In our conversations, she described the ways she has invested into her career as an *escaramuzas*. While her father has helped with the majority of the costs involved in competing as an *escaramuza*, Cielo has also invested the majority of her time to becoming a great competitor. Cielo stated:

> You have to have a lot of time…(laughs)…I'm a little strange because I work on the ranch but I know girls on my team who just come to practice…ask for…ask for attention and that is it. They do not work really… not like me and they have stupid amounts of money. This [being an *escaramuzas*] takes time because you have to get everyone working together…but you need money. It is not for everyone…Not for the girl…the girl with no money (laughs). I have girlfriends in the past that liked what I did but realized that it was impossible for them. *Escaramuzas* are not inviting people. They want to know who you are…
>
> (Interview, 2014)

Cielo is referring to the exclusive nature of the *escaramuzas* she has competed with her whole life. Similar to the discriminatory practices of generational charro cowboys towards charro cowboy rookies, *escaramuzas* without generational ties are rare. This is not because there is no interest but rather there is no feasible entry point. The majority of *escaramuzas* without generational ties are rich women with a connection to charro cowboy *jefes*. Access in these cases is achieved because the newcomer can pay their way on to the team. This does not mean, however, that these women do not face resistance by generational *escaramuzas*. However, money does guarantee newcomers with a place on the team unlike the experiences of charro cowboy rookies who are subjected to dangerous positions or strenuous labor in order to pay their participation costs. Unlike charro cowboy events, the majority of the *escaramuzas* events require performances to be done in unison. While there are some roles of authority on the team, *escaramuzas* must learn to perform team routines rather than entering individual events. The only individual event that exists is a modified version of the *cala de caballo*, in which *escaramuzas* must demonstrate their horsemanship skills. Participation in these events, however, is reserved for the most skilled charro cowboy women. Newcomers are rarely given the opportunity to perform in this individualized event.

*Escaramuzas* are not welcoming to people who question the charro cowboy tradition. This was evident in my observations and during the interview process with these women. Due to their high ranking position in the charro cowboy community, my position as researcher threatened their belief in the charro cowboy tradition because I asked them to verbalize issues they often ignored (i.e. sexism, classism, and racism). They were highly selective about who they talked to during *charreadas*, but *escaramuzas* that did agree to be interviewed revealed why they felt animosity towards outsiders. Similar to the way that charro cowboys are the keepers of the charro cowboy tradition, *escaramuzas* maintain, enact, and reproduce the ideals of charro cowboy female respectability. Outsiders, especially female outsiders, may use charro cowboy men to evaluate their status or as an access point to the charro cowboy community, a point that I referred to in Chapter 4. Their animosity is strongly evident against poor women with indigenous ties. One particular *escaramuza* argued that these women do not belong in the charro cowboy community because they are bad for the bloodlines. This type of rationale is bounded to notions of racism and exclusion against indigenous communities in Mexico. The reference of bloodlines by *escaramuzas* indicates the socialization from birth for women to date and marry men of lighter complexion. This again is a continuous contradiction of the original ethos of the charro cowboy tradition where emphasis was placed on opportunity for all and the resistance against racial and ethic distinctions.

Many of *escaramuzas* that compete in the charro cowboy community are lighter in complexion, in addition to coming from families with a higher socio-economic status. Although the issue of colorism (distinctions within ethnic and racial groups based on the shade of one's skin) is a general social problem through Mexico, this is exacerbated in the charro cowboy community. This may be because women in the charro cowboy community are expected to give birth to the next generation of charro cowboys. As referred to in Chapter 4, high ranking charro cowboy women must be wary of who they date and engage in romantic relationships with, therefore becoming more selective about their romantic partners. Due to *escaramuzas'* cultural connection to Spanish elements of female aristocracy, issues of cultural and ethnic superiority are intensified. For example, Renata, a 31-year-old *escaramuzas* with generational ties, explained that *escaramuzas* should remain a high-class group. Renata stated:

> [Participating as *Escaramuzas*] should remain for women like me. We have real connections to the [charro cowboy tradition]. Not everyone is going to be displayed in the same way on the horse. You have to be feminine...you have to blend in...be together. You can always tell who does not belong.
> Betty: How can you tell?
> Renata: (Laughs)...well...because they look like people on the street.
> (Interview, 2014)

Renata was inferring to women with darker complexions. Although Renata is a college educated mother of two, her ideological standpoint on who can be an *escaramuzas* is clear. During our interview, she specified that women with darker complexions do not look "right" riding next to women with lighter complexions. Despite the fact that Renata's statements are by far the most problematic and racist, she presents a common assumption of the charro cowboy community: charro cowboy women with lighter complexions are better than those with darker complexions. By integrating these schools of thought as to how *escaramuzas* view access to their teams, it evident that *escaramuza* teams are even more selective than charro teams. This selectivity is based on what the charro cowboy community expresses as beautiful and elegant. There is little room for gender nonconforming individuals or even people from marginalized communities to participate. The reputability that is produced from the conspicuous consumption of *escaramuzas* is therefore limited to certain participants. Women of darker complexions and different ethnic backgrounds are excluded because they are still associated with lower levels of employment and social status.

Furthermore, the beauty and graceful nature of the *escaramuza* should not be mistaken as effortlessness. On the contrary, the equestrian technique required for these performances requires continuous dedication and practice. Any miscalculation in the routine may result in collision and injury to riders and animals. Riding side saddle also requires training. Cielo stated, "It's all about balance with your body. Shifting your weight… it can result with ending on the floor." Cielo learned how to ride side saddle when she was five because her mother taught her. Nevertheless, further training was provided by her father who hired a coach to teach her how to maneuver her horse. Rosario, a 20-year-old generational charro cowboy female family member, was also trained by a paid coach. Rosario's mother was not an *escaramuza* but her father's sisters were when they were teenagers. Her father hired the most expensive coach in order to ensure that Rosario would have a place on a popular team in Mexico. Rosario explained that the majority of the women she competed with were like her. She stated:

> They have family in [the charro cowboy community]. I have known some of them from the events that our fathers have and from the different associations that come to [Mexico City]. A few of my teammates went to high school with me…(laughs). This is an expensive sport…you need the money to compete. We happen to have it.
>
> (Interview, 2015)

Rosario went to an expensive private high school in the Federal District. She alluded to her father's wealth as her source of access to the *escaramuza* participation and believes *escaramuza* teams should not accept everyone. Unlike the charro cowboy men who still claim that the charro cowboy tradition is not discriminatory based on class, *escaramuzas* recognize that the cost of participation may not be accessible to everyone.

The women who participate as *escaramuzas* are often perceived to be the most beautiful women at *charreadas*. They are required to enhance their femininity through the use of makeup and hair products. For example, it takes an average of an hour to an hour and half for *escaramuzas* to get ready for events. Rosario explained that she has to make sure that her makeup matches the rest of her teammates' makeup. There are often disagreements about how makeup should be done but the majority of *escaramuzas* wear heavy eyeliner to accentuate the color of their eyes, neutral tone eye shadow, pink blush, and a bright red lipstick. Their hair is long and is normally brushed back into a ponytail or in a braid to avoid getting hair in their faces during their performances. Similar to charro cowboy competitions, *escaramuzas* are also judged by a group of judges who are also appointed by the Mexican Federation of Charros and who have competed in the past as *escaramuzas* and charros. Judges evaluate *escaramuzas* not just by their performance but also their appearance therefore, it is important to make sure that *escaramuzas* to look uniformly beautiful.

Veblen (1899) described the focus on beauty as a "canon of honorific waste". It serves no function in society other than to display wealth, time, and honor. *Escaramuzas* must adhere to these canons of honorific waste because it demonstrates how much money and time goes into their performance. When arguing about the descriptions of women in Homeric poems, Veblen stated:

> But there are certain elements of feminine beauty, on the other hand, which come in under this head, and which are of so concrete and specific a character as to admit of itemized appreciation. It is more or less a rule that in communities which are at the stage of economic development at which women are valued by the upper class for their service, the ideal of female beauty is a robust, large-limbed woman. The ground of appreciation is the physique, while the conformation of the face is a secondary weight only.
>
> (Veblen 1899, 67)

The charro cowboy community, on the other hand, values small waists and slender bodies. Some *escaramuzas* expressed extreme pressure to lose weight or keep their hair long, even though they preferred alternative styles. This was definitely the case of Cielo, who wanted to cut her hair short in a man's style since she was 12. Beauty, as Veblen (1899) argued is visible, an obvious implication of temperament, taste, propensity, and lifestyle. Any form of deviation is obvious.

In short, *escaramuzas* are usually wealthy women with generational ties to the charro cowboy community. They do not accept newcomers who lack the financial stability to invest in the lavish demands of *escaramuzas* teams, nor the "right look" to participate. Veblen's theoretical framework regarding the barbaric and the peaceable can be examined in *escaramuzas* teams. The barbaric Spanish aristocracy intertwined in the participation of *escaramuzas* clearly illustrates how the charro cowboy tradition can be exclusionary based on race and class. While not all *escaramuzas* are as harsh regarding race and class, these discriminatory practices still exist in the charro cowboy community. *Escaramuzas* believe that participation should be selective, yet secondary to men in the charro cowboy tradition.

## Self-reflection and charro cowboy scrutiny

*Escaramuzas* believe that their performances are important to the charro cowboy tradition. They believe that their participation celebrates a cultural past significant to Mexico's notion of nationalism. The *escaramuzas* were incorporated formally into the *charreadas* in the 1960s and many *escaramuzas* are pleased with this inclusion because it presents them with the opportunity to display their equestrian skills in addition to their high level of femininity. Rosario believed that the *escaramuzas* are not above charro cowboy men in the charro cowboy tradition since *charreadas* celebrate Mexican equestrian skills dawning from the charro cowboy tradition. She recognized that the charro cowboy tradition is not centered around women but expressed that *escaramuzas* have their own moments during *escaramuzas* competitions. She said, "No one comes to see just us. The most exciting part is the *charreada*." She did not say this with disappointment or a sense of resentment. She believes that the *escaramuzas* present a particular subset of Mexican femininity. "I work hard but not as hard as [charro cowboy men]. My life is not about being a charro cowboy like them." Rosario is complicit in her own subordination to the charro cowboy tradition because that is how she was socialized. Her mother and grandmother told her from a young age that being an *escaramuzas* would be a fun activity since her brothers were learning to be charro cowboys. No generational charro cowboy views their own participation as a hobby.

The idea that *escaramuzas* are secondary in relation to competing charro cowboys is echoed by Cielo. While she rejects many of the hypermasculine ideologies about the role of women in the charro cowboy community, she still acknowledges that *Escaramuzas* are not respected by charro cowboy men. Cielo stated:

> I have [charro cowboy] friends tell each other when they mess up that they were going to try out for *escaramuzas*. They like to look at us but they do not care for what we do. We are just there to look at... (laughs) but who wants to look at them (laughs).

It was not uncommon to hear charro cowboy men insult each other by calling each other *escaramuzas* for failing to perform well during a competition. Cielo described an important issue in the performances of *escaramuzas*, the presentation of women as trophies. As I have referenced previously, Veblen argued:

All the women in the group will share in the class repression and depreciation that belongs to them as women, but the status of women taken from hostile groups has an additional feature. Such a woman not only belongs to a subservient and low class, but she also stands in a special relation to her captor. She is a trophy of the raid, and therefore and evidence of exploit, and on this ground it is to her captor's interest to maintain a peculiarly obvious relation of master toward her.

(Veblen 1899, 507)

The notion that women are trophies is very much present in the charro cowboy community. The financial burden that is placed upon the charro cowboy fathers of many of the *escaramuzas* establishes that charro cowboy men are exhibiting their daughters and wives. Their wealth provides the opportunity for these *escaramuzas* to look flawless in public but also to exhibit mastery of skills funded by their affluence. The ability to spend money on your daughter or wife to participate is in conjunction with the emerging charro cowboy leisure class described in Chapter 1. As Veblen argues, the purpose of funding this expensive activity is not only to enact, reproduce, or maintain the role of *escaramuzas* in the charro cowboy community, but also to elevate the status of charro cowboy men who are able to promote their honor and prestige. There is no *escaramuza* tradition, only a charro cowboy tradition; *escaramuzas* are only a component of the charro cowboy tradition that celebrates elements of the past.

*Escaramuza* competitions are divided into two categories. The first feature of the competition requires *escaramuzas* to perform a modified *cala de caballo* (reining demonstration). Young women are expected to race their horses from the far end of the lienzo to a reined stop with a sliding stop. Depending on the competition, *escaramuzas* may be required to perform spins to be evaluated on their reining capabilities. This is the only portion of *escaramuzas* performances that vaguely reflects the performances of charro cowboys. However, *escaramuzas* have to do this demonstration side saddle, which makes it more difficult. The gendered distinction in the performance further illustrates how men and women in the charro cowboy community are categorized differently. The second feature of the competition requires *escaramuzas* to enact drill maneuvers to the tune of traditional Mexican music. The performance requires *escaramuzas* to be in unison, thereby making any mistake obvious to the judges and the audiences. In particular, performances that incorporate the *cruzada* demonstrate the highest discipline and grace. Performances that incorporate *cruzada* moves can be explained as a threading needle action. *Escaramuzas* riders ride in lines and alternate crossing other lines of galloping horses. This feature of the competition is unique to *escaramuzas*.

Although charro cowboys and *escaramuzas* share similar competition features, charro cowboys do not respect them as true competitors. Many charro cowboys have used the words, "pretty" and "cute" to describe *escaramuzas* and their competitions. These expressions demonstrate how little value charro cowboy place on *escaramuza* events. As Cielo mentioned above, charro cowboy men do not take the *escaramuzas* performances seriously, for example, the older generation of charro cowboys use the term *escaramuzas* to stigmatize their peers for lower quality performances. Samuel, the 51-year-old generational charro cowboy, was the most vocal about telling other charro cowboys, in particular young charro cowboys, that they should look at careers as *escaramuzas*. During one particular *charreada*, Samuel was drinking coke and tequila with a few of his friends. One charro cowboy from the opposing team had missed his third opportunity in the *colas en le lienzo* or the steer tailing of a bull. Samuel stated to his friend, "Look, another *escaramuzas* for your daughter's team." These comments continued throughout the night. By comparing these low performing charro cowboys to *escaramuzas*, charro cowboy men conceptualize that *escaramuzas* do not have the skills necessary to be compared to them.

These comments may seem insignificant but demonstrate how *escaramuzas* are not truly equal participants in the charro cowboy tradition. They are only for display. Veblen argued:

> In such a community the standards of merit and propriety rest on an invidious distinction between those who are capable fighters and those who are not. Infirmity, that is to say incapacity for exploit, is looked down upon. One of the early consequences of this deprecation of infirmity is a tabu on women and on women's employments. In the apprehension of the archaic, animistic barbarian, infirmity is infectious. The infection may work its mischievous effect both by sympathetic influence and by transfusion. Therefore, it is well for the able-bodied man who is mindful of his virility to shun all undue contact and conversation with the weaker sex and to avoid all contamination with the employments that are characteristic of the sex.
>
> (Veblen 1899, 504)

Veblen's analysis of women in barbaric and predatory cultures, those with a highly present patriarchal structure, provides clarity of the role of *escaramuzas* in the charro cowboy community. By saying that low performing charro cowboys "should try out for *escaramuzas*", Charro cowboys are claiming that they exhibit characteristics of the subordinate class (women). *Escaramuzas* are for display and not for the purpose of exhibiting brute, prowess, and charro cowboy excellence. These elements are absent from the *escaramuzas* performances.

The younger generation of charro cowboys tend not to be as vocal about their thoughts regarding their views of *escaramuzas*. Nevertheless, they do still make such comments. While there are many factors that can contribute to a charro cowboy's desire to perform well (i.e. to maintain their contract with a charro cowboy *jefe*), avoiding stigmatization from their peers plays an important role. Stigma is usually in the form of jokes that imply that charro cowboy men are not performing well.

During one of their competitions, Santiago had had a great night in the *charreada*. His team had won the overall *charreada* and had qualified to go to an important qualifying regional competition; yet, one of his teammates, Joan did not perform to his potential. Joan, usually, is an exceptional charro cowboy and the majority of his teammates believe that he is one of their best charro cowboys. Joan is a 27-year-old generational charro cowboy and specializes in the *colas en le lienzo* or the steer tailing of a bull. During that particular *charreada*, Joan failed to obtain the majority of the points because his hand was slipping off the bull's tail. He had previously broken his finger during practice and had trouble fully closing his hand. Despite his injury, Joan still generated a middle-level score that was able to help propel his team to victory. Santiago, knowing that Joan had broken his finger, jokingly suggested that if his career as a charro cowboy continued to deteriorate he should look into joining an *escaramuzas* team. Although annoyed with Santiago, Joan laughed and said that he would rather die than join an *escaramuzas* team. Santiago responded by stating that Joan would look horrendous in a dress anyway so he recommended that Joan had better get well quickly before he was faced with that option.

*Escaramuzas* are fully aware that charro cowboys use their identity as a form of stigmatization. While most are annoyed that charro cowboys do not view their equestrian skills as legitimate, there is not much that *escaramuzas* can do to combat this form of discrimination. Violeta, a 35-year-old *escaramuza* with generational ties stated, "If they did not respect the original *escaramuzas*, they are not going to respect us." Violeta, unlike Renata and Rosario, views her participation as an *escaramuza* as just as important to the charro cowboy tradition as charro cowboy men and the *suertes charras*. While Violeta is an outlier to her peers, her point regarding the treatment of *escaramuzas* remained valid. She said, "My own brothers say that what we do is so easy…(laughs)…easy…like easy (laughs)…You try riding with your weight on one side." Violeta's frustration stems from years of hearing her brothers use the term *escaramuzas* to mean stigmatization. While some *escaramuzas* may wish to be honored in the same way that charro cowboy men are in the charro cowboy community, a majority of *escaramuzas* are "deal with" the reality that they will never be paramount in the charro cowboy tradition.

## Mexican Federation of Charros and their relationship with *escaramuzas*

As I argued in Chapter 1, the Mexican Federation of Charros has become the voice and keeper of the charro cowboy tradition. The participation of *escaramuzas* became a favorable addition to *charreadas* once former President Carlos Pascual and governing board of the Mexican Federation of Charros were encouraged by experienced *escaramuzas* to form a council of judges. By 1989, the Mexican Federation of Charros had formalized a set of rules for competition specifically for *escaramuzas*. Sands stated in her analysis of *escaramuzas*, "Before these women drew up competition rules and certified judges, there were *escaramuzas* competitions, but they did not lead to tournaments or titles. The informal competitions were organized and judged exclusively by charros who had no consistent system of scoring" (Sands 1993). The need for regulation and standardization led to the emergence of an all-female *Escaramuzas* Council of Judges. This was an important step for *escaramuzas* because it motivated *escaramuzas* teams to perfect their skills. Former Vice President José Luis González of the Mexican Federation of Charros believed that *escaramuzas* competitions were important to improve the quality of *escaramuzas'* performance.

Although there are a lot more options for competitions today, *escaramuza* teams still prefer to compete alongside charro cowboy men because of the lack of attendance of their performances otherwise. While there was a push for all-women judges, in my observations of *escaramuzas* competitions, the majority of judges only included one female judge while the other judges were usually older experienced charro cowboys. The Mexican Federation of Charros incorporated *escaramuzas* with charro cowboy competitions because there are not as many *escaramuzas* teams registered in the Mexican Federation of Charros. Once again, this is due to the cost and heavy financial burden associated with *escaramuzas* teams. Charro cowboy teams with a wealthy charro cowboy *jefe* tend to have a "sister" *escaramuza* team and travel with the charro cowboy team when there is an opportunity to compete. This is due to the high cost to travel from one area to another with *escaramuzas* horses. This is because most charro cowboy horses and *escaramuzas* horses require different types of training, both being costly.

*Escaramuzas* make *charreadas* even more festive and colorful. The Mexican Federation of Charros recognize that a profit can be made for exhibiting *escaramuzas* alongside charro cowboy men during major competitions. Framed under Veblen's understanding of predatory instincts and habits, there is an incentive for charro cowboy *jefes* and financiers to exploit *escaramuza* teams because they have the greatest means to pay. Owners of *lienzos* that are used for major regional competitions and championship competitions charge an additional fee to have *escaramuzas*. They create an incentive for *escaramuzas* to compete by promising them money and equipment as first prize, similar to charro cowboy men. Additionally, the top competitors are always invited back to major competitions that are well advertised in the charro cowboy community. This incentive is strong enough to motivate charro cowboy *jefes* to fund *escaramuza* teams alongside their charro cowboy teams. Further, the scheduling of the charro cowboy competition is also impacted by *escaramuza* competitions because when *escaramuzas* are performing, charro cowboy teams can prepare their horses for the latter part of the competition and get lunch or dinner with their teammates. The Mexican Federation of Charros is strategic with how they utilize the *escaramuzas* in their major competition. While they may present themselves as inclusive to *escaramuzas*, they are incentivized by profit not equality.

*Escaramuzas* are not aware of how their representation in the Mexican Federation of Charros is organized. Many do not know that they are not included in the ballots for major decisions centered on the preservation of the charro cowboy tradition. Like many charro cowboys, they do not question the authority of the Mexican Federation of Charros because they believe they have their best interests at heart. *Escaramuzas* do not have formal representation in the Mexican Federation of Charros, but they do have a symbolic role. Every few years, the Mexican Federation of Charros elect a young *escaramuzas* as the Queen of the Mexican Federation of Charros. These women are almost always wealthy, of high status, and generational. The election resembles more of a pageant where women are evaluated on their beauty rather than their contributions to the charro cowboy tradition. Their generational connections play an important role in their selection, as well-known charro cowboy families carry more weight in these decisions than other charro cowboy families. Here, the Mexican Federation of charro cowboys can present the illusion that *escaramuzas* are valued for their skills rather than their beauty.

Former queens of the Mexican Federation of Charros are required to take many professional photographs in full *escaramuzas* attire. They are not known for their skills, but rather their beauty. They are present in major competitions to wave the flag of the Mexican Federation of Charros and they ride their horses alongside the President and Vice President of the Federation. They may take pictures with the competition winners but they do not have a role in judging competitions. *Escaramuzas* believe that the queens of Federation represent them, but they are unsure of her role. Out of the ten *escaramuzas* that I interviewed, not one could tell me what the Queen of the Mexican Federation of Charros did. The representatives that I interviewed from the Mexican Federation of Charros stated that the Queens of the Mexican Federation of Charros were suppose to serve at least two terms and their job was to "proudly represent the ladies of horsebacks, the charro cowboys, and the national sport." Their statements did not clarify her duties but rather what the Queen of the Mexican Federation of Charros symbolizes to their organization.

The inclusion of *escaramuzas* limits their participation to just beauty, grace, and respectability in the charro cowboy community. There are some women in the charro cowboy community that do wish to participate on the same level as men, but they are a small minority. They are pushed back by the Mexican Federation of Charros because many representatives of the Federation believe that women do not have the capacity to portray the charro cowboy tradition in the manner in which it was intended. Lucero, a 25-year-old with generational ties to the charro cowboy community, learned how to do the *suertes charras* secretly when she was a child. She is a former *Escaramuzas* and would like to compete alongside men. Lucero mentioned that she can do anything that a charro cowboy can do, but no one has given her the opportunity to display her skills. She said:

I have to be secretive about who I talk to about [my skills]. My father did not know about it for years and he caught me on the ranch one day…trying to do [Piales en Lienzo or Heeling of a running mare]. He was pissed…(laughs) but then he forgot about it. Mom tells me it is not right…it is not feminine. That is why I quit being an *escaramuza*… (laughs)… too feminine. I have tried to get other *escaramuzas* to join me but no one seems to want to do this with me.

(Interview, 2014)

Lucero's family is not supportive but her brother, Marco has helped her practice. Not many women wish to participate alongside men because many charro cowboy men and women believe the charro cowboy tradition should not be altered to include women. Many say that this is why *escaramuzas* were incorporated into *charreadas* in the first place.

In 2016, there was a small and controversial informal event for charro cowboy women interested in performing two of the charro cowboy events. This event took place in Mexico City and was not widely advertised; nevertheless, it served as a potential entry point for skilled women in the charro cowboy community. These women did not wear dresses, but rather the classic charro cowboy attire. Charro cowboy women who participated were supervised and were watched by volunteer judges who helped them correctly execute the events, *Piales en Lienzo* and the *Colas*. The women who participated had generational ties to the charro cowboy community. Although this was the first competition of its type, I have yet to see another of its kind. Scholars interested in this culture will have to continue to document these changes as more women become verbal about wanting to participate in the charro cowboy tradition. These changes, however, will not be easy and may take decades.

The role of *escaramuzas* in the charro cowboy community can be understood as a form of conspicuous consumption. Wealthy charro cowboy families are able to further display their power and money through the participation of their female family members in this exclusive group. Participation in *escaramuzas* is limited, not because of the lack of interest, but rather the financial and racial barriers that exist, making it hard for outsiders of different backgrounds to feasibly join these teams. *Escaramuzas* are required to be beautiful, perform in unison, and be subordinate to charro cowboy men. The manner in which charro cowboy men use the term *escaramuza* as a form of stigma is evidence of how the *escaramuza* remains secondary to the charro man. *Escaramuzas* will continue to be exploited by those with predatory and barbaric habits as long as their inclusion produces honor, profit, and prestige.

## Note

1 The role of the *escaramuza* in the charro cowboy community is comparable to the American National Football League's cheerleaders. Although an integral part of the National Football League's revenue stream, cheerleaders are paid (sometimes below) minimum wages and are required to attend unpaid events. In a recent 2016

court case, the NFL's Buffalo Bills cheerleaders, known as Buffalo Jills, sued and successfully won a case between the NFL's team for wage inequality. The Buffalo Jills made claims about requirements of strict dress codes and guidelines that were regulated by the NFL's Buffalo Bills. These are not the first claims and lawsuits that have occurred in the NFL regarding the treatment of their female dancers. These court cases further illustrate how women in sport, specifically in traditionally masculine sports, are seen as symbolic.

## References

Ancona, George. *Charro: The Mexican Cowboy*. San Diego: Harcourt Brace. 1999.

Chávez Torres, Guillermina. "La Comunidad Transncional Tamuzulense: Relaciones socioculturales e interacción comunicativa off/online." Dissertation thesis, Department of Social Sciences, Centro Universitario de Investigaciones Sociales, 1998.

Davis, Henry. "For Jills, something to cheer about: Judge rules they were employees." *The Buffalo News*, May 19, 2017. Accessed July 2017 https://buffalonews.com/2017/05/19/judge-decides-jills-lawsuit-employees-not-independent-contractors/.

López, Esteban Barragán. *Con un pie en el estribo: Formación y Deslizamientos de las Sociedades Rancheras en la Construcción del México Moderno*. Zamora, Michoacán: El Colegio de Michoacán AC. 1997.

Medina, Héctor M. "Charros and Bullfights on Both Sides of the Atlantic Ocean: Folkloric Stereotypes and Traditional Festivals between Myth and History." *Folklore*, vol. 126 (2015): 68–88.

Miranda, Héctor M. Medina. *Los charros en España y en México: estereotipos ganaderos y violencia lúdica*. Salamanca, España: Instituto de Identidades, Diputación de Salamanca. 2013.

Montfort, Ricardo Pérez. *Expresiones populares y estereotipos culturales en México, siglos XIX y XX: diez ensayos*. México, D.F.:Ciesas. 2007.

Nájera-Ramírez, Olga. "The Charreada in the United States." In *Art of Charrería: A Mexican Tradition*, 17–21. Los Angeles: Autry Museum of Western Heritage. 2002.

Nájera-Ramírez, Olga. "Discursos Transnacionales Sobre la Charreada, La Violencia y lo Mexicano." In *Las Nuevas Fronteras del Siglo XXI: Dimensions Culturales, Políticas y Socioeconomicas de las Relaciones México-Estados Unidos*, eds. Alejandro Alvarez Béjar, Norma Klahn, Frederico Manchón and Pedro Castillo, 195–210. Mexico: La Jornada Ediciones. 2000.

Nájera-Ramírez, Olga. *Engendering Nationalism: Identity, Discourse and the Mexican Charro*. University of California, Santa Cruz: Chicano/Latino Research Center. 1993.

Nájera-Ramírez, Olga. "Haciendo Patria: The Charreada and the Formation of a Mexican Transnational Identity." In *Transnational Latina/o Communities: Politics, Processes, and Culture*, eds. Carlos Velez-Ibanez and Anna Sampaio, 167–180. Boulder, CO: Rowan and Littlefield Press. 2002.

Nájera-Ramírez, Olga. "Mounting Traditions: The Origin and Evolution of the Escaramuza Charra." In *Chicana Traditions: Continuity and Change*, eds. Norma E. Cantú and Olga Nájera-Ramírez, 207–223. Champaign, Illinois: University of Illinois Press. 2002.

Nájera-Ramírez, Olga. "The Racialization of a Debate: The Charreada as Tradition or Torture?" *American Anthropology*, vol. 98 (1993): 505–511.

Ramírez Barreto, Ana Cristina. "Defendiendo animales, redefiniendo tradiciones. Cómo charros y charras en California enfrentan las acciones legales contra eventos de la charreada." In *De humanos y otros animals,* 195–199. México:Editorial Dríada. 2009.

Sands, Kathleen M. *Charrería Mexicana: An Equestrian Folk Tradition.* Tucson: University of Arizona Press. 1993.

Valero Silva, José. *El Libro de la Charrería.* Mexico City: Gráficas Montealbán. 1989.

Veblen, Thorstein. "The Barbarian Status of Women." *American Journal of Sociology, vol.* 4, no. 4 (1899): 503–514.

Veblen, Thorstein. *The Theory of the Leisure Class: An Economic Study of Institutions.* New York: Reprint by The New American Library. 1953[1899].

# 6   Conclusion

Thorstein Veblen, a prominent sociologist, economist, and cultural critic, provides an important sociological perspective to the dynamics of rural traditions. The collective of his work may remain predominately unknown and unused by cultural theorists in sociology, yet Veblen's contributions remain useful in unraveling the shifts in rural cultures. Although neglected by the majority of sociology, Veblen's arguments centered on predatory and barbaric habits remain a relevant issue for analysis of the changing character of rural tradition and all agricultural-based societies. Although Veblen's analysis served to be important in the examination of American culture, his theoretical framework extends beyond the United States. Riesman (1953) extended Veblen's significance as a cultural theorist beyond the United States, thereby extending the potential of his theoretical framework in other areas of analysis. The charro cowboy tradition presents itself as an acceptable case study of the barbaric and predatory habits that are taking over its practices. The examination of race, class, and gender was possible with sociological work. However, clarity was achieved through the use of Veblen's analysis of gradual changes in society due to capitalism and influences of modernity.

The charro cowboy tradition in this book was condensed and not all of my ethnographic work could be included. The previous four chapters focused on the applicability of Veblen's work to ethnographic case studies like the charro cowboy community. The methodology of this book involved in-depth participatory observations and interviews that allowed for a clearer picture of how the charro cowboy community functioned and was structured . The first chapter introduced the importance and value of Veblen's vast work. While Veblen has not generally been considered to be an ethnographer, like his peers at the University of Chicago, his formation of his theories suggests that observations are important to understand the surrounding cultural environment. In addition, the first chapter introduced the history and national significance of the charro cowboy community to enable the reader to understand how Veblen and the charro cowboy community intersect. I delineated, briefly, the complex history of the charro cowboy community in order to pinpoint the peaceable and barbaric elements that were already in place during its inception. Further, assessing these important foundational beliefs of the charro cowboy community were crucial to highlighting the current contradictions of the modern charro cowboy community regarding brotherhood, freedom, and continuation of oppressive practices.

Chapter 2 examined the analysed the influence of business principles in the charro cowboy community. Mexico, as a country, has a clear entrepreneurship and capitalistic spirit, nevertheless, current business practices of the charro cowboy demonstrate a clear shift in cultural habits and forego the quasi-peaceable expectations to maintain one's livelihood. Business practices go beyond the peaceable to the barbaric and predatory habits that promote exploitation for honor, prestige, and status. In this chapter, I argued that charro cowboy *jefes* operated their teams in an exploitative fashion, for the benefit of their own status rather than the re-enactment and reproduction of the charro cowboy tradition. Further, the standardization of the charro cowboy tradition had a great impact on the manner which charro cowboys enacted their equestrian skills and why they decided to compete in the charro cowboy tradition and also on the welfare of charro cowboys and their animals. Veblen's understanding of the parental bent and instinct of workmanship was useful in framing the prominent predatory and barbaric habits of the charro cowboy who engages heavily in charro cowboy business principles. I noted differences in generations of charro cowboys that placed importance on trophies rather than solely the continuity of their tradition because of the influence of the growing charro cowboy leisure class. Ultimately, I argued that charro cowboy business principles played an important role in the rift between the older generation and younger generation of charro cowboys.

Chapter 3 analysed the socialization of generational charro cowboys and how they constructed their identity. Veblen's *Theory of the Leisure Class* (1899) was imperative to the analysis of class and racial differences in the charro cowboy community. Counter to the charro cowboy tradition, generational ties became synonymous with authenticity. I examined the class differences that promoted the discrimination of lower class generational charro cowboys due to their lack of resources. Lower class generational charro cowboys therefore enacted predatory and barbaric practices against newcomers or charro cowboy rookies. The rise of a wealthier charro cowboy leisure class allowed for lower class charro cowboys to use "bloodlines" as a means to exclude newcomers and to elevate their status. Further, I looked at the experiences of charro cowboy rookies and revealed that race-based discrimination played a role in the integration of these newcomers. These elements of discrimination revealed the contradictions with the very ideology of the charro cowboy tradition. I argued that charro cowboy rookies with indigenous ties experienced higher incidents of marginalization and acts of exclusion, a clear contradiction of the original intention of the charro cowboy tradition.

Chapters 4 and 5 focused on the role of women in the charro cowboy community. Chapter 4 focused on the ranking of women and was framed using Veblen's "The Barbarian Status of Women" (1899). His particular understanding of women in barbaric and predatory cultures was necessary to examine how charro cowboy women are continuously marginalized. I examined class, gender, and race-based discrimination that placed generational wealthy women at the top of the social hierarchy and lower class indigenous women at the bottom. Women in the charro cowboy were separated into three different categories: 1) charro cowboy female family members; 2) charro cowboy love interests; and 3) female outsiders, *vendedoras*. Respectability and manners are at the forefront of social dynamics among high ranking women. Respectability ensures membership in the community, in addition to positively benefiting the charro cowboy men that they represent. A pattern of respectability and decency plagued the charro cowboy women and failure to conform threatened their reputation and the reputation of their charro cowboy families. Charro cowboy love interests, particularly temporary love interests, elevated the status and honor of men. Temporary love interest failed to gain the respect of charro cowboy men because they lacked the cultural knowledge to be respected. Female outsiders were important elements of this analysis to demonstrate the treatment of the lowest ranking women. I argued that the ranking of women in charro cowboy community is testimony to their barbarian status.

The final chapter, Chapter 5, revealed that the inclusion of *escaramuzas* in the charro cowboy tradition remains symbolic and is a clear indicator that women in the charro cowboy community remain subordinate to men. The role of *escaramuzas*, I argued, can be interpreted as a form of conspicuous consumption due to the requirement to be beautiful and wealthy. *Escaramuzas* competitions are exclusive and participation is limited to wealthy and honorable families. While it may be honorable for charro cowboy family members to have their women participate in the community, charro cowboy men use the term *escaramuza* as a derogatory term form charro cowboy men who fail to meet the expectations of their peers. The derogatory use of the *escaramuza* further shows how women in the charro cowboy community are secondary to men. Further, the Mexican Federation of Charros' use of the *escaramuza* as a potential source of revenue demonstrates the continuous use of predatory and barbaric habits to produce honor, profit, and prestige.

In conclusion, the use of Veblen remains valuable in the assessment of ethnographic research. Although the case study of this book is a rural tradition in Mexico, Veblen's cultural analysis remains relevant and important. While Veblen's most famous work, *Theory of the Leisure Class* (1899) is the most popular, I ask his followers and other cultural theorists to look beyond this to see his potential in providing their cultural research with a well-rounded background. The shifts of the peaceable and the barbaric can illuminate arguments that could not have been visible without the use of Veblen. My hope is to provide a reader with the tools necessary to include Veblen in contemporary cultural sociology and ethnographic work on rural traditions.

This study merged the contributions of Thorstein Veblen to examine the work of the charro cowboy tradition, however, his work could uncover other types of cultural phenomena not examined in this book. Future research on the charro cowboy tradition might examine the increasing standardization of the charro cowboy tradition by the Mexican Federation of Charros, which is increasingly powerful and ever growing. Its power and profit centered agenda will continue to impact how the charro cowboy community enacts, reproduces, and maintains the charro cowboy tradition. In addition, the element of sexual orientation was only briefly mentioned here. Gay charro cowboys do exist but remain marginalized and subjected to high levels of stigmatization if they disclose their identities to other members of the community. Some gay Charro cowboys are threatened with violence by other charro cowboys while being encouraged by others to remain silent about their identities. Research on sexuality and non-conforming members would be a crucial component on this complex rural tradition and would reveal contradictions within structures of hegemonic masculinity. The mechanisms in which social media is changing the mechanisms in which charro cowboys share their tradition with others should also be evaluated in future investigations. Furthermore, the community's desire to survive, regardless of a changing Mexico, should be investigated to document if survival is possible or if the charro cowboy tradition will submit to a new and more modern Mexico.

## References

Riesman, David. *Thorstein Veblen*. New York: Charles Scribner's Sons. 1953.

Veblen, Thorstein. "The Barbarian Status of Women." *American Journal of Sociology*, vol. 4, no. 4 (1899): 503–514.

Veblen, Thorstein. *The Theory of the Leisure Class: An Economic Study of Institutions*. New York: Reprint by The New American Library. 1953[1889].

# Index